BLOOD ATONEMENT
AND
THE ORIGIN OF PLURAL MARRIAGE

LECTOR HOUSE PUBLIC DOMAIN WORKS

HAPPY READING!

BLOOD ATONEMENT
AND
THE ORIGIN OF PLURAL MARRIAGE

JOSEPH FIELDING SMITH, JR.,
RICHARD C. EVANS

ISBN: 978-93-5420-781-5

Published: -

© 2021
LECTOR HOUSE LLP

LECTOR HOUSE LLP
E-MAIL: lectorpublishing@gmail.com

BLOOD ATONEMENT
AND
THE ORIGIN OF PLURAL MARRIAGE
A DISCUSSION

Correspondence between ELDER JOSEPH F. SMITH, (JR.,) of the Church of Jesus Christ of Latter-day Saints, and MR. RICHARD C. EVANS, second counselor (1905) in the Presidency of the "Reorganized" Church. A conclusive refutation of the false charges persistently made by ministers of the "Reorganized" Church against the Latter-day Saints and their belief. Also a supplement containing a number of affidavits and other matters bearing on the subjects.

"To correct misrepresentation, we adopt self representation."

—John Taylor.

CONTENTS

INTRODUCTION

The correspondence in this pamphlet was brought about through the wilful misrepresentation of the doctrines of the Latter-day Saints and the unwarranted abuse of the authorities of the Church by Mr. Richard C. Evans, in an interview which appeared in the Toronto (Canada) *Daily Star* of January 28, 1905. A copy of the interview was placed in the hands of the writer, who, on February 19th following, replied to Mr. Evans in an open letter which was published in the Toronto Star on or about the 25th of the month.[1] This open letter was answered by Mr. Evans in a personal letter, and on the 23rd of May, a rejoinder to his reply was sent to Mr. Evans at his home in London, Ontario, Canada. In all, four communications—including the interview—have passed between us, and all of these four communications are here reproduced *in full*. A copy of the open letter which appeared in the *Star*, was also sent to Mr. Evans who acknowledged its receipt. Nothing more was done in regard to this correspondence until August 17th and 24th, when an article containing a portion of it appeared in the *Zion's Ensign*, published by the "Reorganized" church at Independence, Jackson County, Missouri, under the title: "Statements Authenticated," in which it was made to appear that the full and complete communications were reproduced. But this, however, was not the case.

In a letter from Mr. Evans to the editor of the *Ensign* which accompanied the above mentioned article, he said:

> Believing that good will be accomplished by the publication
> of the entire matter, I herewith mail you the referred to matter.

From this it would naturally be supposed that the *complete* correspondence would be given. However I was not surprised to see that Mr. Evans' side of the controversy was *in full*, while a large portion of my first communication had been purposely suppressed; and that my second letter *did not appear at all!* And thus was the *"entire matter"* given to the readers of the *Ensign* that "good" might be "accomplished." (?)

The parts that were purposely left out of my communication by Mr. Evans, were most vital to the subject and have been indicated as they appear in the body of this work by being placed in italics, excepting a few minor matters which he omitted that I have not mentioned, nevertheless matters that throw light upon the subject.

---

[1] As I did not receive a copy of the *Toronto Star* I cannot positively say that my article appeared in full, but if it did not Mr. Evans is still without excuse for not considering the *entire matter* for he received personally a duplicate copy of the article sent the *Star* which contained those portions he has failed to include in his "entire matter" in the *Zion's Ensign*.

One of these quotations was in relation to two articles in the first volume of the *Saints' Herald* which were important, coming, as they did from the "enemy's" camp. Here is the omitted part:

> If you believe your statement to be true, will you kindly explain the following passage in the *Saints' Herald*, your official organ, volume I, page 9,—it would be well for you to read the entire chapter, which is entitled "Polygamy." The quotation is as follows:

> "The death of the Prophet is one fact that has been realized, although he abhorred and repented of this iniquity (meaning "polygamy") before his death. This branch of the subject we shall leave to some of our brethren, who are qualified to explain it satisfactorily."

> In the same volume, page 27, what is meant by the following: "He, (Joseph Smith) caused the revelation on the subject (polygamy) to be burned, and when he voluntarily came to Nauvoo and resigned himself into the arms of his enemies he said that he was going to Carthage to die. At that time he also said that if it had not been for that accursed spiritual wife doctrine he would not have come to that." Kindly read the context.

> There is more evidence that can be produced, but if you will explain this it may suffice.

The first half of the succeeding paragraph was quoted but the second half was omitted. I quote in full with the part suppressed in italics:

> In the light of the knowledge I have received and the evidence at my command, I know that the Prophet Joseph Smith made no such statement as the above, and that he did not have the revelation burned. *There is, however, value in the above statements from your "Herald," for they bear witness to the origin and introduction of the principle of plural marriage and revelation concerning the same.*

It is easy to perceive that Mr. Evans felt "that good will be accomplished by the publication of the 'entire matter'"; and for that reason he omitted this evidence which the leaders of the "Reorganization" have been trying so successfully to destroy for lo these many years. The two articles in the *Saints' Herald* have caused the leaders of that sect no end of trouble, and today they are in the same fix in regard to plural marriage that the first editor of that paper was when he wrote, for they cannot explain the Prophet's connection with the principle "satisfactorily," and never will be able to until they acknowledge the truth.

Another of Mr. Evans' ommissions that "good" might be "accomplished" (?) is the following paragraph in reference to President Brigham Young:

> It is true that President Young was elected president at Kanesville; but on what grounds do you charge him with holding the office in trust for the "dead president's son?" Do you not

know that such a statement —contrary to the written word—was antagonistic to the teachings of President Young, as recorded in the *Times and Seasons*, as well as since that time?

Will you please explain on what grounds you charge President Young with being "under suspicion at the time of Joseph Smith's death?" Am I to infer by this that you mean to convey the idea that Brigham Young was in any way responsible for the death of Joseph Smith? The Prophet never had a truer friend. You know that at the time of the martyrdom Brigham Young was on a mission away from home. If this is the inference you wish to convey, it is not only contemptible but viciously false.

It appears from the actions of many of those who fight the Latter-day Saints, that they fully realize their inability to successfully oppose the doctrines of the Church with truth as a weapon of attack, and, therefore, resort to falsehood, vilification and abuse, attempting to blind those who are not acquainted with the facts. The doctrine of the Church has survived all such onslaughts and continues to spread throughout the earth, as a witness against those who have adopted such base methods for its overthrow. It will continue to spread, bless mankind and prepare all who accept it, and follow its teachings in righteousness, for an inheritance in the kingdom of God.

The Reorganite ministers are generally in the front rank among those who oppose the Church and resort to tactics of a doubtful character. They travel from place to place, never losing an opportunity in private, on the rostrum or through the press, to "explain the radical difference" between their organization and that of the Church of Jesus Christ of Latter-day Saints, and in denouncing "the Utah Mormon and his iniquities." On such occasions they will quote garbled and isolated extracts from sermons and from writings by Elders of the Church, taking particular pains to cover up the context in order to prejudice the uninformed mind. In this way many a harmless, inoffensive passage has been made to do great execution in some quarters and among a certain class. Nor is this all. Nearly every crime that was committed within a thousand miles of Utah in early days and many that were invented out of whole cloth, are brought to bear against the "dreadful Mormons," the Church and the Gospel, that they may be stigmatized and made to appear vile and hateful before the world. So much of their time is spent in this way that they can surely have but little left in which to tell the world what they themselves believe.

No reason except that of misrepresentation and jealousy can be assigned for actions of this kind. These men oppose the truth in a spirit of jealousy and to cover up their own false position, and by such an attitude prove that they are ashamed of their own faith, being conscious of its weakness.

The supplement following the correspondence is composed of a number of affidavits and other testimony bearing on the subjects under discussion, which, it is hoped, will be of interest and perhaps of value to the reader.

JOSEPH F. SMITH, JR.

Salt Lake City, Utah, September 5, 1905.

MR. R. C. EVANS' INTERVIEW IN THE TORONTO, CANADA, "DAILY STAR," JAN. 28, 1905

LATTER-DAY SAINT VISITING TORONTO—MR. R. C. EVANS, WHO IS PROMOTING THE GROWTH OF HIS CHURCH IN CANADA, NOT A BELIEVER IN POLYGAMY—DENOUNCES THE UTAH MORMONS.

The name Mormon does not please Toronto's six hundred baptized Latter-day Saints, not to mention the fifty thousand others scattered over the globe.

This fact was emphasized today, when R. C. Evans, one of the three members of the Presidency, explained the radical difference between the two denominations. Mr. Evans, who reached Toronto a few days ago to spend a month here, denounces the "Utah Mormon and his iniquities."

"We do not believe in polygamy, blood atonement, and kindred evils," he said to the *Star* last night at 142 Peter street, where he is visiting, "They are an abomination to the Lord. The term Mormon is offensive to us, because it is associated in the public mind with the practices that I have specified. The other night, while I was holding a service here, four Utah Elders came to me. I referred to polygamy, and they defended it. 'We endorse it,' they told me, 'but we don't practice it.' Three women were with them, and I said to one, 'Do you believe in polygamy?' 'I do,' she replied, 'and I know that God will punish the United States for prohibiting it.' I understand that there are five Utah elders in Toronto at the present time, and in addresses here I will expose polygamy and blood atonement."

BORN NEAR MONTREAL

Mr. Evans is forty-three years old, but doesn't look his age. He is rather below medium height, strongly built, wears his black hair short, and his round, slightly olive face is clean shaven. He is animated in manner, and though his English is occasionally at fault, he speaks fluently and well. He was born at St. Andrew's near Montreal, but his ancestry is not confined to any one country, Irish, Welsh and German blood flows in his veins and his somewhat nasal voice is typically American.

"I was baptized in 1876," he said, "ordained a priest in 1882, became an elder in 1884, entered the quorum of seventy in 1886, was chosen one of the twelve apostles in 1897; and in 1902, was selected one of President Joseph Smith's two counselors, the other being his eldest son, Frederick M. Smith. I was the pastor of the London, Ontario, church from 1882 to 1886, and have given particular attention to Canada. We occupy a rented church on the corner of Sumac and St. David streets, a new church on Camden street, and another at Humber Bay, practically three congregations in Toronto."

The Latter-day Saints and the Utah Mormons, according to Mr. Evans, are frequently confused, greatly to his regret.

TROUBLES OF THE SECT

"My President Joseph Smith," he explained, "is the oldest son of Joseph Smith, who, when a boy of fifteen, was directed to the mound wherein he found the golden plates from which he compiled the Book of Mormon.

"He organized his church in 1830, when 25 years old, and between 1830 and 1844 his following numbered 200,000. In 1844 he was shot and killed for his anti-slavery sympathies,[2] and with him died his brother Hyrum. John Taylor, a Toronto convert of 1838, was wounded, but recovered. Joseph Smith's city of Nauvoo, Illinois, was wrecked, and in 1847, at Kanesville, Iowa, Brigham Young was elected president, though he still professed to hold the office in trust for the dead president's eldest son, also, Joseph, whom the father had consecrated as his successor.[3] Brigham Young reorganized[4] the church, rebaptized every member, including himself, and in 1848 (1847) he reached Salt Lake City. With him went the widow and children of Hyrum Smith, whose son Joseph F., is now president of the Utah church. The widow of the first president had refused to follow Young, and her boy Joseph was brought up in his father's footsteps, hating polygamy and other impurities. 'Young Joseph,' as he was called, connected himself with the Saints, who had rejected Brigham Young, and was elected their president. He was then 28 years old. In 1872 he was called to Washington, a report having reached the Government that Mormonism had again sprung up in Illinois. He disproved the charge of polygamy and blood atonement, and demonstrated that Latter-day Saintism was in keeping with the law and supported by the Bible. Incorporation was granted, and we have prospered.

---

[2] Mr. Evans' declaration that the Prophet was killed for his anti- slavery sympathies is rather surprising, when we consider that he was in one of the anti-slave states, and the mob at Carthage was largely composed of men with very strong "anti-slavery sympathies." The fact is he and his brother Hyrum were martyred for their religion of which Celestial Marriage, (including Plural Marriage) formed a part. One of the charges made against them was that of teaching "polygamy."

[3] In proof that the Prophet did not ordain or consecrate his son as his successor, the reader is referred to the affidavits of John W. Rigdon and Bathsheba W. Smith.

[4] As the Church was never disorganized, it could not be reorganized. Mr. Evans has made a mistake. It was the Quorum of the First Presidency that was disorganized at the Prophet's death and which was *reorganized* when Brigham Young was elected President, and not the Church.

UPHELD DEATH

"Brigham Young, who had been under suspicion at Joseph Smith's death, introduced polygamy and blood atonement at Salt Lake City. Blood atonement meant death to anyone who left his church. Brigham Young's argument was that the apostate whose throat was cut from ear to ear, the favorite way, saved his soul, but his object was to keep his people under his iron heel. Young was a shrewd, bad man.

"I spent a day and a half with Joseph F. Smith at Salt Lake City three years ago, and he gave me a group photo of himself, his surviving five wives, and thirty-six children. His first wife was dead. She died broken-hearted and insane. Personally, Joseph F. Smith is a genial, kindly man, but he and I differed on Polygamy. I told him it was vile and wicked, always had been, and always would be. In appearance he resembles his cousin, my own president."

Mr. Evans is married, and has two children. The three faces look at you from his watch case. He has recently returned from the northwest. His faith has several thriving churches there, he says, while the Utah Mormons are settled in one part of Alberta.

REPLY TO R. C. EVANS

The following letter was published in the Toronto *Daily Star* in answer to the false charges which appeared in Mr. Evans' interview.

Salt Lake City, Feb. 19, 1905.

Mr. R. C. Evans,
Counselor in Presidency of Reorganized Church.

Sir:—I have before me a copy of the Toronto *Daily Star*, bearing date of January 28, last, in which there is a column on the front page, purporting to be an interview, by a representative of that paper with you, in which I desire to call your attention.

In doing so I desire to be fair and dispassionate, and also candid, and I would like it if you would receive and reply to this communication in the same spirit and manner to me personally.

You are reported as not being "pleased," nor Toronto's six hundred baptized members, with the name "Mormon." "This fact," says the *Star*, "was emphasized today when R. C. Evans, one of the three members of the Presidency explained the radical difference between the two denominations. Mr. Evans * * * denounced the Utah Mormon and his iniquities." Then you are made to say: "The term Mormon is offensive to us, because it is associated in the public mind with the practices that I have specified." That is, the alleged practices of the Utah "Mormons," namely, "polygamy and blood atonement."

Did you know that "the term Mormon" has always been applied to the Church of Jesus Christ of Latter-day Saints? That the name attached to the Church with the publication and promulgation of the Book of Mormon? That it was first applied by the enemies of the Church as an opprobrium; but that during the lifetime of Joseph Smith the Martyr, and ever since it has been a term accepted by the Church because of popular custom, as an appellation?

If, then, the name is so distasteful to you and your fellows in Canada and throughout the world, although it be on the grounds you have named, why do you not discard the Book of Mormon, from whence the name is derived, as well as the name. Is not the term *Book of Mormon* as closely associated in the public mind with "polygamy and blood atonement," as is the *name* of the Book? How are you going to disassociate the book itself from the name as commonly applied to the Church, since this name has been attached to the Church from the beginning, and before the alleged "practices" of the "Utah Mormon" gained such publicity? *Really, I think it would be quite proper for those holding the view which you are said to have expressed, not only to renounce the name "Mormon" as applied to the Church but also the Book itself.*[5]

You do not believe in blood atonement. Is not this the more reason why you should discard the Book of Mormon? Are you not at issue with the teachings not only of that book, but also with those of the Bible on this matter? If so, why not discard the Bible, and while you are about it, the Book of Doctrine and Covenants also? Both of these, as well as the Book of Mormon, teach the doctrine of "blood atonement," and they are all "associated in the public mind" with the alleged "practices" of the Church of Jesus Christ of Latter-day Saints.

Let us consider this subject of "blood atonement."

Book of Mormon:

Mosiah 3:11.—His blood atoneth for the sins of those who have fallen by the transgression of Adam. Verse 15.—And understood not that the law of Moses availeth nothing except it were through the atonement of his blood. Verse 16.—Even so the blood of Christ atoneth for their sins.

Alma 21:9.—Now Aaron began to open the Scriptures unto them concerning the coming of Christ, and also concerning the resurrection of the dead, and that there could be no redemption for mankind, save it was through the death and suffering of Christ, and the atonement of his blood.

I Nephi 12:10.—Their garments are made white in his blood.

II Nephi 9:7.—And if so, (not an infinite atonement) this flesh must have laid down to rot and to crumble to its mother earth, to rise no more.

From the Bible:

Mark 14:22-25.—And as they did eat, Jesus took bread and blessed and brake it, and gave to them, and said: Take, eat; this is my body.

And he took the cup, and when he had given thanks, he gave it to them: and they all drank of it.

And he said unto them, This is my blood of the new testament which is shed for many.

Verily I say unto you, I will drink no more of the fruit of the vine, until that day that I drink it new in the Kingdom of God.

From the Doctrine and Covenants:

Section 45:4.—(Utah edition) Saying, Father, behold the sufferings and death of him who did no sin, in whom thou wast well pleased; behold the blood of thy Son which was shed—the

---

[5] This sentence in italics was omitted in Mr. Evans' publication of the *entire matter* in the *Zion's Ensign*, August 17th, 1905.

blood of him whom thou gavest that thyself might be glorified.

Section 74:7.—But little children are holy, being sanctified through the atonement of Jesus Christ, and this is what the scriptures mean.

Section 76:39-41.—For all the rest shall be brought forth by the resurrection of the dead, through the triumph and the glory of the Lamb, who was slain, who was in the bosom of the Father before the worlds were made. And this is the gospel, the glad tidings which the voice out of the heavens bore record unto us. That he came into the world, even Jesus, to be crucified for the world, and to bear the sins of the world, and to sanctify the world, and to cleanse it from all unrighteousness.

Section 29:1.—Listen to the voice of Jesus Christ, your Redeemer, the Great I AM, whose arm of mercy hath atoned for your sins. Verse 17.—And it shall come to pass, because of the wickedness of the world, that I will take vengeance upon the wicked, for they will not repent; for the cup of mine indignation is full; for behold, my blood shall not cleanse them if they hear me not.

STATEMENT OF AN ENEMY

But the report says: "This doctrine was introduced by Brigham Young" and that it meant "death to anyone who left the Church * * * that the apostate whose throat was cut from ear to ear * * * saved his soul." Why you made this statement you best know; but were you not aware that it was but the repetition of the ravings of enemies of the Church, without one grain of truth? Did you not know that not a single individual was ever "blood atoned," as you are pleased to call it, for apostasy or any other cause? Were you not aware, in repeating this false charge, that it was made by the most bitter enemies of the Church before the death of the Prophet Joseph Smith? Do you know of anyone whose blood was ever shed by the command of the Church, or members thereof, to "save his soul?" Did you not know that you were embittering the people against the "Mormon" Elders, and that just such malicious charges and false insinuations have made martyrs for the Church, whose blood does not "cease to come up into the ears of the Lord of Sabaoth?"

Never in the history of this people can the time be pointed to when the Church ever attempted to pass judgment on, or execute an apostate as per your statement. There are men living in Utah today who left the Church in the earliest history of our State who feel as secure, and are just as secure and free from molestation from their former associates as you or any other man could be.

EFFICACY OF THE BLOOD OF CHRIST

The Latter-day Saints believe in the efficacy of the blood of Christ. They believe that through obedience to the laws and ordinances of the Gospel they obtain a remission of sins; but this could not be if Christ had not died for *them*. If you did believe in blood atonement, I might ask you why the blood of Christ was shed? and *in whose stead was it shed*? I might ask you to explain the words of Paul: "Without shedding of blood is no remission."

UNPARDONABLE SINS

Are you aware that there are certain sins that man may commit for which the atoning blood of Christ does not avail? Do you not know, too, that this doctrine is taught in the Book of Mormon? And is not this further reason why you should discard the Book as well as the name? Is it not safe for us to rely upon the scriptures for the solution of problems of this kind? Let me quote:

From the Book of Mormon:

II Nephi 9:35.—Wo unto the murderer who deliberately killeth, for he shall die.

Alma 1:13, 14.—And thou hast shed the blood of a righteous man, yea, a man who has done much good among this people; and were we to spare thee, his blood would come upon us for vengeance.

Alma 42:19.—Now, if there were no law given—if a man murdered he should die, would he be afraid he would die if he should murder?

From the Bible:

Genesis 9:12, 13.—And whoso sheddeth man's blood, by man shall his blood be shed; for man shall not shed the blood of man.

For a commandment I give, that every man's brother shall preserve the life of man, for in mine own image have I made man. (Inspired translation.)

Luke 11:50.—That the blood of all the prophets, which was shed from the foundation of the world, may be required of this generation.

Hebrews 9:22.—And almost all things are by the law purged with blood; and without shedding of blood is no remission.

Hebrews 10:26-29.—For if we sin wilfully, after that we have received the knowledge of the truth, there remaineth no more sacrifice for sins.

*　　　*　　　*　　　*　　　*

He that despised Moses' law died without mercy under two or three witnesses;

Of how much sorer punishment, suppose ye, shall he be thought worthy, who hath trodden under foot the Son of God, and hath counted the blood of the covenant, wherewith he was sanctified, an unholy thing.

(I commend to you the careful reading of these two chapters:)

I John 3:15.—No murderer hath eternal life abiding in him.

I John 5:16.—If any man see his brother sin a sin which is not unto death, he shall ask, and he shall give him life for them that sin not unto death. There is a sin unto death: I do not say that he shall pray for it.

From the Doctrine and Covenants:

Section 87:7.—That the cry of the saints, and of the blood of the saints, shall cease to come up into the ears of the Lord of Sabbath, from the earth, to be avenged of their enemies.

Section 101:80.—And for this purpose have I established the constitution of this land, by the hands of wise men, whom I raised up unto this very purpose, and redeemed the land by the shedding of blood.

Section 42:18, 19.—And now, behold, I speak unto the church. Thou shalt not kill; and he that kills shall not have forgiveness in this world, nor in the world to come.

And again, I say, thou shalt not kill; but he that killeth shall die.

Verse 79.—And it shall come to pass, that if any persons among you shall kill, they shall be delivered up and dealt with according to the laws of the land; for remember that he hath no forgiveness, and it shall be proved according to the laws of the land.

THE LAW OF CAPITAL PUNISHMENT

In pursuance of, and in harmony with this scriptural doctrine, which has been the righteous law from the days of Adam to the present time, the founders of Utah incorporated in the laws of the Territory provisions for the capital punishment of those who wilfully shed the blood of their fellow man. This law, which is now the law of the State, granted unto the condemned murderer the privilege of choosing for himself whether he die by hanging, or whether he be shot, and thus have his blood shed in harmony with the law of God; and thus atone, so far as it is in his power to atone, for the death of his victim. Almost without exception the condemned party chooses the latter death. This is by the authority of the law of the land, not that of the Church. This law was placed on the statutes through the efforts of the "Mormon" legislators, and grants to the accused the right of jury trial. It is from this that the vile charge, which you are pleased to repeat, has been maliciously misconstrued by the enemies of the Church, who prefer to believe a lie. When men accuse the Church of practicing "blood atonement" on those who deny the faith, or, for that matter, on any living creature, they know that they bear false witness, and they shall stand condemned before the judgment seat of God.

PLURAL MARRIAGE

Since the action taken by the United States government, and also by the Church, in regard to plural marriage, I shall not discuss its virtues nor answer arguments in opposition to that principle as a principle of our faith. As you, however, are reported to have said that "Brigham Young introduced" that doctrine "in Salt Lake City," I would be pleased if you would explain, as a matter of history, why Sidney Rigdon, before "President Young introduced" the doctrine, declared that the principle of plural marriage was introduced, to his knowledge, by Joseph Smith the Prophet, and that he, Sidney Rigdon, rejected that doctrine and "warned Joseph Smith and his family" that it would bring ruin upon them. You will find this in the *Messenger and Advocate*, published in June, 1846, volume 2, page 475, number 6. Will you kindly explain why this same Sidney Rigdon practiced polygamy, which he so fervently condemns? Will you kindly explain why Lyman Wight, James J. Strang, Gladden Bishop, William Smith, and others, none of whom had much love for President Young and did not follow him, also taught and practiced polygamy *before plural marriage was "introduced by President Young."* If you doubt this, I will gladly furnish you with the proof. Indeed, you may find a great deal of it in the third volume of your church history.

THE "SAINTS' HERALD" AS A WITNESS

If you believe your statement to be true, will you kindly explain the following paragraph in the *Saints Herald*, your official organ, volume 1, page 9. It would be well for you to read the entire chapter, which is entitled "polygamy." The quotation is:

"The death of the prophet is one fact that has been realized, although he abhorred and repented of this iniquity (meaning 'polygamy,') before his death. This branch of the subject we shall leave to some of our brethren, who are qualified to explain it satisfactorily."

In the same volume, page 27, what is meant by the following?

"He (Joseph Smith) caused the revelation on the subject ('polygamy') to be burned, and when he voluntarily came to Nauvoo and resigned himself into the arms of his enemies he said that he was going to Carthage to die. At that time he also said that if it had not been for that accursed spiritual wife doctrine, he would not have come to that." Kindly read the context.

There is more evidence that can be produced, but if you will explain this it may suffice.

In the light of the knowledge I have received and the evidence at my command, I know that the Prophet Joseph Smith made no such statement as the above, and that he did not have the revelation burned. *There is, however, value in the above statements from your "Herald," for they bear witness to the origin and introduction of the principle of plural marriage, and the revelation concerning the same.*[6]

[6] The quotations from the *Saints' Herald* which are in Italics were purposely omitted from Mr. Evans' "publication of the entire matter," as it appeared in the *Zion's Ensign* of August 7, 1905. The reason for the suppression of this evidence is easy to discern. The authorities of the "Reorganization" have tried to destroy the evidence, that it could not be circulated among their church members, therefore very few copies of this particular *Herald*

THE UTAH VISIT

In connection with this, let me call your attention to your visit to Salt Lake City some three years ago. At that time you met President Lorenzo Snow, a man whose veracity cannot justly be questioned; you heard him bear his testimony to the effect that he was taught that principle by the Prophet Joseph Smith, and that the Prophet declared to Lorenzo Snow that he had married his sister, Eliza R. Snow. You met and conversed with Lucy Walker Smith, and she told you that she was married to the Prophet Joseph Smith on the first day of May, 1843, in Nauvoo, Elder William Clayton performing the ceremony. You met Catherine Phillips Smith, who told you she was married in August, 1843, in Nauvoo, to the Patriarch Hyrum Smith, his brother Joseph the Prophet officiating in that ceremony. You will remember that the first wives of both these men were living at the time. I hardly think these testimonies have passed from your memory in so brief a time. I am personally acquainted with these women, and know that they are truthful and honest—honorable women, whose testimonies should be believed.

In the face of all this evidence, do you think it fair and consistent for you and your fellow believers to constantly lay at the door of President Young the responsibility for the "introduction of plural marriage" and the "authorship" of the above mentioned revelation?

My letter is already long, but I desire to briefly mention another item or two.

PRESIDENT SMITH'S DENIAL

In the interview you are made to say that while on your visit to Salt Lake City, you spent a day and a half with Joseph F. Smith; that you and he "differed on polygamy," and that you "told him it was vile and wicked, always had been, and always would be." I took occasion to ask my father if you and he had discussed polygamy at that time and if you had uttered that above expression or any other of like nature. He replied that he had no discussion with you on that subject; that you did not say one word to him in relation to polygamy, either favorable or otherwise; that your visit was a social one, and friendly, and was not occupied by the discussion of any differences which may have existed.

It is true that President Young was elected president at Kanesville, but on what grounds do you charge him with holding the office in trust for the "dead president's son?" Do you not know that such a statement—contrary to the written word—was antagonistic to the teachings of President Young, as recorded in the "Times and Seasons," as well as since that Time?

PRESIDENT YOUNG THE PROPHET'S FRIEND

Will you please explain on what grounds you charge President Young as being "under suspicion at the time of Joseph Smith's death?" Am I to infer by this that you mean to convey the idea that Brigham Young was in any way responsible for the death of Joseph Smith? The Prophet never had a truer friend. You know that at the time of the martyrdom Brigham <u>Young was on a mission away from home. If this is the inference you wish</u> to convey, it is can today be found.

not only contemptible but viciously false.[7]

With reference to my father's first wife, you say she died "broken hearted and insane." If you mean to insinuate that this condition, if true, was the result of any act whatever on the part of my father, it is also scandalously false. I have good reason to believe that she died neither broken hearted nor insane. If it were true, I would still think that you, as a professed minister of the Gospel, might employ your time to better advantage than as an aspersor or a scandal-monger.

Respectfully,
Joseph F. Smith, Jr.

[7] These paragraphs in italics were also omitted from Mr. Evans' "publication of the entire matter," as it appeared in the *Zion's Ensign* August 17, 1905.

MR. EVANS' LETTER

Mr. Joseph F. Smith, Jr.:

Sir:—Your open letter published in the Toronto *Star* for February 25, is before me. You say: "I desire to be fair, dispassionate and also candid." Those who read your letter will see plainly that you have mispresented the interview, my faith and the facts concerning my visit to Salt Lake, and that you are guilty of a labored effort to cover up the *true facts* regarding "blood atonement," "polygamy," etc., and my faith in the Book of Mormon. So much for those desires.

My position with regard to the Book of Mormon, and the name "Mormon," is too well known for you to blind the people concerning it. The interview shows plainly in what sense "the term 'Mormon' is offensive to us." Read it again, sir: "Because it is associated in the public mind with the practices that I have specified." The abominations of *Brighamism*; namely, polygamy, blood atonement, Adam-God,[8] and other evils that have disgraced the name throughout civilization.

------

[8] The teachings of the Latter-day Saints in relation to the doctrine of the Godhead are clearly set forth in Elder B. H. Roberts' valuable work, "Mormon Doctrine of Deity." For the belief of the "Mormon" people regarding Adam and his place in the universe, attention is called especially to chapters one, five and six of that work; also to Doctrine and Covenants, sec. 78:15-18, sec. 107:53-57 and Daniel 7:9-14. In relation to this matter I quote the following from the remarks of President Anthon H. Lund delivered at the General Conference, October 6, 1902.

"Some there are who follow our Elders, and after they have preached the principles of salvation, these men get up and charge that the Elders do not believe in God, but that they believe in Adam as their God, and they will bring up a few passages from sermons delivered by this or that man in the Church to substantiate this charge. Now, we are not ashamed of the glorious doctrine of eternal progression, that man may attain the position of those to whom came the word of God, that is gods. When Jesus was preaching unto the Jews on one occasion they stoned Him, and He wanted to know if they stoned Him for the good works He had been doing. Oh, no, they say, 'for the good work we stone thee not; but for blasphemy; and because that thou, being a man, makest thyself God.'"

He quoted the 33rd to 37th verses of the 10th chapter of the Gospel of St. John, and said:

"We believe that there are gods as the Savior quoted. He repeated what was written in the law, and he did not say that it was wrong, but used it as an argument against them (The Jews.) While, however, we believe as the scripture states, that there are more gods, to us there is but one God. We worship the God that created the heavens and the earth. We worship the same God that came to our first parents in the Garden of Eden. In the revelation contained in section 116 of the Book of Doctrine and Covenants the Lord speaks concerning Adam-ondi-Ahman, 'the place where Adam shall come to visit his people, or the ancient of days shall sit, as spoken of by Daniel the Prophet.' In the 107th section the Lord speaks

The true Church never has adopted the name "Mormon" as being the proper name of the church. The Latter-day Saints were sometimes called "Mormons" in derision, as you admit, because they believed in the divine authenticity of the Book of Mormon, and some church members may have been willing to be called "Mormon"; yet you "candidly (?) fairly, dispassionately" ask me, "Why do you not discard the Book of Mormon from whence the name is derived?" Now, sir, I profess to believe in the divine authenticity of the Holy Bible; as well call me a Bible, because I believe in the Bible,[9] as call me a Mormon because I believe in the Book of Mormon.

The church that I have the honor to represent is incorporated under the laws of the United States as "The Reorganized Church of Jesus Christ of Latter Day Saints."

BLOOD ATONEMENT

There is not an honest thinking person on earth who is acquainted with the faith of the church regarding the atonement of Jesus Christ but that will say your attempt to misrepresent my faith in this regard is diametrically opposite to your stated desire to be "fair, dispassionate and candid." You know that a prominent article in the Epitome of the Faith and Doctrine of the *true church* reads as follows: "We believe that through the atonement of Christ, all men may be saved by obedience to the laws and ordinances of the gospel." You know that the true church believes in the atoning blood of Christ as stated in the scriptures you cite in your letter, and yet you try to make out that because we do not believe in the doctrine of blood atonement as taught by Brigham Young and his successors in "Utah Mormonism," that we do not believe in the atonement of our Lord and Savior Jesus Christ.

The doctrine of the atonement of Christ is far above the doctrine of blood atonement as taught by Brighamism. To prove this, I submit the statements as made by Brigham Young and other leading members of the Utah Church, as found in their sermons, printed by your church:

Brigham Young said, October 9, 1852: "What shall be done with the sheep that stink the flock so? We will take them, I was going to say, and cut off their tails two inches behind their ears; however I will use a milder term, and say cut off their

of Adam as Michael, the Prince, the Archangel, and says that he shall be a prince over the nations forever. We may with perfect propriety call him Prince, the Ancient of Days, or even God in the meaning of the words of Christ, which I have just quoted. When our missionaries are met with these sophistries and with isolated extracts from sermons we say to them anything that is a tenet of our religion must come through revelation and be sustained by the Church, and they need not do battle for anything outside of the works, that have been accepted by the Church as a body."

[9] If popular custom had designated the true believers of the Bible as "Bibles" as a term of distinction from other worshippers, there is no reason why a true believer should be offended even at that appellation but rather honored. Mr. Evans, without doubt, is not ashamed of the name "Christian," yet this term, like that of "Mormon" was first applied to the followers of Christ in derision, "because it was associated in the public mind with the practices" of the early Saints, which practices in that day were looked on as "abominations."

ears."—Journal of Discourses, vol. 1:213.

Brigham said again, March 27, 1853: "I say, rather than that apostates should flourish here, I will unsheath my bowie knife, and conquer or die. (Great commotion in the congregation and a simultaneous burst of feeling, assenting to the declaration.) Now, you nasty apostates, clear out, or judgment will be put to the line and righteousness to the plummet. (Voices generally, 'Go it, go it.') If you say it is all right, raise your hands (all hands up). Let us call upon the Lord to assist us in this and every good work."—Journal of Discourses, vol. 1:83.

Echoing what Brigham said, P. P. Pratt said, on March 27, 1853, "My feelings are with those who have spoken, decidedly and firmly so. * * * I need not repeat their doom, it has been told here today, they have been faithfully warned. * * * It is too late in the day for *us* to stop and inquire whether such an outcast has the truth."—Journal of Discourses, vol. 1, pp. 84, 86.

Elder Orson Hyde said April 9, 1853: "Suppose the shepherd should discover a wolf approaching the flock, what would he be likely to do? Why, we would suppose, if the wolf was within proper distance, that he would kill him at once * * * kill him on the spot. * * * It would have a tendency to place a terror on those who leave these parts, that may prove their salvation when they see the heads of thieves taken off, or shot down before the public."—Journal of Discourses, vol. 1:72, 73.

President Brigham Young preached, February 8, 1857, as follows "All mankind love themselves; and let these principles be known by an individual and he would be glad to have his blood shed. That would be loving themselves even to an eternal exaltation. Will you love your brothers and sisters likewise when they have committed a sin that cannot be atoned for without the shedding of blood? That is what Jesus Christ meant. He never told a man or woman to love their enemies in their wickedness. He never intended any such thing.

"I could refer you to plenty of instances where men have been righteously slain in order to atone for their sins. I have seen scores and hundreds of people for whom there would have been a chance in the last resurrection if their lives had been taken and their blood spilled upon the ground, as a smoking incense to the Almighty, but who are now angels to the devil, until our elder brother, Jesus Christ, raises them up, conquers death, hell and the grave.[10] I have known a great

------

[10] This is a misquotation, it should be: "I could refer you to plenty of instances where men have been righteously slain, in order to atone for their sins. I have seen scores and hundreds of people for whom there would have been a chance (in the last resurrection there will be) if their lives had been taken and their blood spilled on the ground as a smoking incense to the Almighty, but who are now angels to the devil, until our elder brother Jesus Christ raises them up—conquers death, hell and the grave."

In that same discourse President Young declares that those who were "righteously slain" were the wicked that the "Lord had to slay" in ancient Israel. There is not one word in that discourse to indicate that those who were slain to "atone for their sins" were killed in Utah; but to the contrary they were ancient inhabitants of the earth, viz., the antediluvians who perished in the flood, the inhabitants of Sodom and Gomorrah, of Jericho and the cities destroyed by the Israelites; the prophets of Baal whom Elijah slew (I Kings 18:40) and a host of others of that class and the class to whom the one belonged of whom the Savior said: "It

many men who have left this church, for whom there is no chance whatever for exaltation; but if their blood had been spilt it would have been better for them. The wickedness and ignorance of the nations forbid this principle being in full force, but the time will come when the law of God will be in full force.

"This is loving our neighbor as ourselves; if he needs help, help him; and if he wants salvation and it is necessary to spill his blood upon the ground in order that he may be saved, spill it." — Journal of Discourses, vol. 4, p. 220, or Deseret News, vol. 6, p. 397.

President J. M. Grant said, September 21, 1856: "I say there are men and women here that I would advise to go to the president immediately, and ask him to appoint a committee to attend to their case, and then let a place be selected, and let that committee shed their blood." — *Deseret News*, vol. 6, p. 235.

President Heber C. Kimball said; July 19, 1854: "It is believed in the world that our females are all common women. Well, in one sense they are common—that is, they are like all other women, I suppose, but they are not unclean, for we wipe all unclean ones out of our midst; we not only wipe them from our streets, but we wipe them out of existence. And if the world wants to practice uncleanness, and bring their prostitutes here, if they do not repent and forsake their sins, we will wipe the evil out. We will not have them in this valley unless they repent, for so help me God, while I live I will lend my hand to wipe such persons out, and I know this people will." — *Deseret News*, August 16, 1854, and *Millennial Star*, vol. 16, pages 738-9.

The above statements speak for themselves, and these were what I read to the reporter. You ask, "Do you *know* of anyone whose blood was ever shed by the command of the church or members thereof to save his soul?" To *know* by hearing such a command given, or seeing a murder committed, is one thing, to believe the evidence of many who have testified is another. No sir, I was never present when such a command was given, nor when murder was committed; but I have read that which leads me to believe that under Brighamism, Utah was for years a land of assassination and a field of blood. What of the Mountain Meadow massacre— the destruction of the Aiken party; the dying confession of Bishop J. D. Lee; the Hickman butcheries; the Danties? Alfred Henry Lewis, writing in *Collier's Weekly* for March 26, 1904, states: "Brigham Young invented his destroying angels, placed himself at their head, and when a man rebelled, *he had him murdered*, if one fled the fold he was pursued and slain."

The world has recently read the testimony of persons under oath, in Washington, who testified concerning the endowment oaths, so I will forbear any further remarks on this subject.

---

were better for him that a millstone were hanged about his neck, and that he were drowned in the depth of the sea." President Young's remarks agree with those of Peter when he declared that the Jews who were guilty of assenting to the crucifixion of Christ could not be baptized nor have their "sins blotted out" until the "times of refreshing shall come," which was at the time of the "restitution of all things." — Acts 3:19-21.

POLYGAMY

Speaking of "plural marriage," you say, "I shall not discuss its *virtues*." Surely that is kind. Let civilization give ear, Mr. Smith calls that a virtue which wrecks the happiness of every woman who is enslaved by it, that doctrine which permits Brighamites to live in what they call marriage with three sisters at one time, with mother and daughter at the same time. Your father, Joseph F. Smith, married and is now living with *two sisters as wives*. I refer to Julina Lambson and Edna Lambson, both bearing children to him; yet you call that system a *virtue*.

I have no evidence that those men you refer to, as having practiced polygamy *before Young was guilty, as stated by you.* But the following evidence shows clearly that Brigham Young was under suspicion before Joseph's death, and that he has since admitted that he had a revelation on polygamy before the church knew anything of the doctrine:

In a speech of Brigham Young on June 21, 1874, (see *Deseret News* of July 1, 1874), we read the following statement relative to the origin of this doctrine of polygamy:

> While we were in England (in 1839 and 1840, I think) the Lord manifested to me by vision and His Spirit, things that I did not then understand. I never opened my mouth to anyone concerning them, until I returned to Nauvoo; *Joseph had never mentioned this; there had never been a thought of it in the church* that I ever knew anything about at that time;—but I had this for myself and kept it for myself.—The Messenger, volume 1, page 29.

Well, no one need blame Joseph any more, Brigham is the self-confessed channel through which polygamy was given to his people.

I here submit the testimony of Brigham Young's legal wife, who left him after he was untrue to her. Testimony of Major Thomas Wanless, given to R. C. Evans, his nephew, in the presence of Mrs. Wanless, Mrs. Evans and her daughter, in St. Louis, Missouri, September 7, 1904:

> I met Brigham Young's first and legal wife and her daughter in the winter of 1860 and 1861, at Central City, Colorado; she told me that Joseph Smith had nothing to do with polygamy; that he did not teach, practice, or in any way endorse the doctrine of polygamy, that he had nothing to do with the so-called revelation on celestial marriage; that he had but one wife. My husband, Brigham Young, Orson Pratt (she gave the name of another man whose name I have forgotten) made up the revelation on celestial marriage.

> Before they left Illinois some of them practiced polygamy. Brigham Young went to Utah to reorganize the church and publicly introduced polygamy, or to reorganize the Church on a polygamous basis.

> She left Brigham Young, finally obtained a divorce from him,

and was then living with her daughter. Brigham sent the daughter money according to an agreement. She told me they ought to have shot Brigham Young in place of Joseph Smith.

This statement of Major Wanless that she was Brigham's first wife is a mistake. Brigham married Miriam Works, October 8, 1824; she died September 8, 1832. In February, 1834, he married May Ann Angel; she was his *legal wife*, and perhaps is the one referred to by the Major. It is quite pardonable in Major Wanless in getting Brigham's wives mixed up. We opine poor Brigham was at his wit's end to keep the family record correct himself.

Chambers' encyclopedia, volume 8, students' edition, confirms Mrs. Young's statement, in part. It says, speaking of the practice of polygamy: "Young, Pratt and Hyde are its true originators. Emma, wife and widow of the prophet, stoutly denied that her husband had any wife but herself. Young's revelation she declared to be a fraud."

From a host of other witnesses who testify that Brigham Young was the man that introduced polygamy in the Church, I submit the statement of another broken-hearted woman from the ranks of Brigham's Church. Fanny Stenhouse says: "Polygamy was unheard of among the (English) Saints in 1849." (pages 45, 47, 48) "Tell It All," by Fanny Stenhouse. "In June 1850, I heard the first whisper of polygamy. In January, 1853, I first saw the revelation on Polygamy; it was published in the *Millennial Star*," (page 132).

"Out of thirty thousand Saints in England in 1853, 1776 had been excommunicated for apostasy through polygamy, the president of the conference was cut off," (page 160). When speaking regarding polygamy she says: "They know that the only source of all their revelations is the man BRIGHAM YOUNG," (page 190).

"Brigham has outraged decency and driven asunder the most sacred ties, by his shameless introduction of polygamy," (page 273).

"There have been many apostates from the teachings of Joseph Smith in early days, but of all apostates, Bro. Brigham is the chief," (page 614).

It is reported by Fanny Stenhouse, and many others, that Joseph Smith said, "If ever the Church had the misfortune to be led by Bro. Brigham, he would lead it to hell," (page 268).

Why did Joseph Smith a short time prior to his death make the above and similar statements regarding the man Brigham Young? The reason is plain. He too had doubtless heard some rumors as to his conduct and secret teachings, and the evidence would seem to indicate that just before his death he made a move to bring the guilty to judgment. We will let William Marks, who was president of the Nauvoo Stake at the time of Joseph Smith's death testify:

"A few days after this occurrence, I met with Bro. Joseph, he said that he wanted to converse with me on the affairs of the Church, and we retired by ourselves; I will give his words *verbatim* for they are indelibly stamped upon my mind. He said he had desired for a long time to have a talk with me on the subject of polygamy. He said it would eventually prove the overthrow of the Church, and we should soon be obliged to leave the United States, unless it could be speedily put down. He was satisfied that it was a cursed doctrine, and that there must be every exertion to put it down. He said that he would go before the congregation and proclaim against it, and I must go into the High Council, and he would prefer charges against those in transgression, and I must sever them from the Church unless they made ample satisfaction. There was much more said, but this was the substance. The mob commenced to gather about Carthage in a few days after, therefore there was nothing done concerning it." (*Saints' Herald*, vol. 1, pp. 22, 23.)

President Marks, after Joseph Smith's death, made mention of the above conversation; it was soon rumored that he was about to apostatize, and that his statement was a tissue of lies." (See *Saints' Herald*, vol. 1, pp. 22, 23.)

Speaking of the revelation on polygamy, Marks said, "I never heard of it during Joseph's life. It was evidently gotten up by Brigham Young and some of the Twelve, after Joseph's death." (Briggs' Autobiography; *Herald* 1901.)

Now I propose to produce evidence showing that Joseph Smith and the Church during his lifetime condemned polygamy in the strongest terms. First, I submit the testimony of thirty-one witnesses as published by the Church on October the 1st, 1842. We deem this sufficient to show you where Joseph and Hyrum Smith stood on this question of polygamy.

"We, the undersigned members of the Church of Jesus Christ of Latter-day Saints, and residents of the city of Nauvoo, persons of families, do hereby certify and declare, that we know of no other rule or system of marriage than the one published from the Book of Covenants, and we give this certificate to show that Dr. John C. Bennett's secret wife system is a creature of his own make, as we know of no such society in this place, nor never did."

This is signed by a number of the leading men of the Church, some of the Twelve Apostles, some of the First Presidency of the Utah Church, and a number of the leading men of the Church. A similar document is signed by Emma Smith the wife of Joseph Smith, and a number of the leading women of the Church, thirty-one witnesses in all.

Now I submit for your consideration a statement made by Joseph Smith and his Brother Hyrum just a few months prior to their assassination. They learned that a man up here in the state of Michigan was teaching polygamy, and this is what they said about it: "As we have lately been credibly informed that a member of the Church of Jesus Christ of Latter-day Saints, a man by the name of Hyrum Brown, has been teaching polygamy and other false and corrupt doctrines, in the county of Lapeer, state of Michigan, this is to notify him and the Church in general that he has been cut off from the Church for his iniquity." Signed, Joseph Smith, Hyrum Smith, Presidents of the Church.

This was given in February, 1844. Joseph was killed four months after that. Here he declares that polygamy is a crime, and the man was excommunicated from the Church for preaching it. Now I want to give you the testimony of George Q. Cannon, whom I met in Salt Lake City, as one of the presidency of the Salt Lake Mormon Church: "A prevalent idea has been that this prejudice against us owes its origin and continuation to our belief in a plurality of wives. * * * Joseph and Hyrum Smith were slain in the Carthage Jail, and hundreds of persons were persecuted to death previous to the Church having any knowledge of this doctrine." —*Journal of Discourses*, vol. 14, pages 165, 166.[11]

This being true, Joseph Smith was not guilty of the practice of polygamy; he was killed before the people knew anything about polygamy. This is the statement of George Q. Cannon. Let me strengthen this now by the son-in-law of Brigham Young, H. B. Clawson:

"Polygamy at that time (that is at the time of Joseph Smith's death) was not known among those of the Mormon faith. * * * The doctrine of polygamy was not promulgated until they got to Salt Lake; not, in fact, until some little time after they had arrived there." Salt Lake *Herald*, February 9, 1882.[12]

Joseph Smith was killed in 1844. They arrived in Salt Lake the 24th of July, 1847, and he says not until some little time after that was it introduced. The little time was the 29th of August, 1852, eight years and two months after the assassination of Joseph Smith.

We have Brigham Young himself on this. He being interviewed by Senator Trumbull in 1869, said: "It (polygamy) was adopted by us as a *necessity* after we came here." Ah, there never was a greater truth told in all the world than that. Polygamy was not an original tenet of the Church, and Brigham Young says it was adopted as a *necessity* after "we came here." The real facts are, Brigham Young, as I will show from their own evidence, and a few other Elders were living vile lives secretly, and to cover up the consequences of their bad conduct, as he truthfully says in this "as a necessity"; yea, as a necessity polygamy was introduced. But who will dare to blame Joseph Smith for their introducing polygamy eight years after his death?

I have been careful to take these clippings right from their own papers, so that they cannot say that we have changed the words or anything of that kind. Here is another statement; this is found from Elder Ephraim Jenson:

"Polygamy was not practiced by the Mormons prior to and at the time of the

---

[11] In extreme haste here to make a point, Mr. Evans left in the middle of a sentence and hurried on to the next page to complete the expression he desired to convey. This is what President Cannon said: "A prevalent idea has been that this prejudice against us owes its origin and continuation to our belief in a plurality of wives; but when it is recollected that the mobbings, drivings, and expulsions from cities, counties and states which we have endured, and our exodus to these mountains all took place before the revelation of that doctrine was PUBLICLY known, it will be seen at once that our belief in it has not been the cause of persecution." Now, I ask, is it not plain to see why his quotation stopped in the middle of a sentence? The Saints all know that President George Q. Cannon was always faithful to his testimony that plural marriage was introduced by the Prophet Joseph Smith. Latter-day Saints generally declare that this doctrine was not *publicly* known in the days of Joseph the Seer, but that it was taught by him to his trusted friends. When this fact is known the alleged quotations which follow, purported to be from H. B. Clawson, Ephraim Jensen and "Elder Whitaker" lose their force.

[12] This is not in the Salt Lake Herald of February 9, 1852.

execution of Joseph Smith, who was executed at Nauvoo, Illinois. * * * Fourth, that only three per cent of the Mormon men practiced polygamy, a proof itself that it was not essential to the creed." — *The Yeoman's Shield.*

Here is another one:

> "Go back to the foundation of our Church, April 6, 1830, there was no polygamy practiced or taught in Mormon literature until five years after that band of persecuted Saints reached Utah." *New York Herald*, January 8, 1900.[13]

This is by Elder Whitaker, who knew who *did* introduce this polygamy. Now I might introduce dozens and dozens of witnesses to prove that Joseph Smith had nothing to do with it. Well, who did it? Here is what the Apostle's wife says of it: "How then, asked the reader, did polygamy originate? It was born in the vile and lustful brain of Brigham Young, and was grafted on the faith to gratify his sensual bestiality."[14] (Mysteries of Mormonism, pp. 16, 17.)

[13] The following is the Brooklyn *Citizen's* report of that same discourse from which Mr. Evans quotes his passage as given in the New York *Herald*: Elder Whitaker said: "The people of the East have been led to believe that polygamy was alone responsible for all the troubles of the Mormons, but the fact remains, that as the fight was waged against Jesus Christ, against his followers, and against all great men for declaring the truth, so the same spirit is manifest now; but the Mormons will humbly seek those willing to accept the truths inspired of God, leaving the justice of their cause to be vindicated by honest investigation and time. The fight is directed against the doctrine of the Mormon Church, though polygamy has done such yeoman service in arousing public sentiment, to attain certain ends unworthy of honest men. The crusaders have kept the public mind from the real cause of the attack. From the time the Church was organized in 1830-47, when the people, after many previous drivings, persecutions, mobbings and cruel mockings, were driven to Utah, the cry of polygamy was never made a cause of their persecutions; indeed, that subject was not committed in writing until 1843, never published to the world until 1852, and was abandoned by the issuance of the 'Manifesto' of President Wilford Woodruff, in 1890, since which time not one polygamous marriage has been solemnized; but those having wives at that time were never asked, and it was never expected they would abandon them, and when death brings such relations to a close, there will be no polygamy among the Mormons." The Brooklyn *Citizen*, Monday, January 8, 1900.

Why Mr. Evans accepted the brief extract from the New York *Herald* in preference to the full account in the Brooklyn *Citizen* will require no comment, but it certainly does appear that Elder Whitaker *did* know who introduced "polygamy."

As I do not have the Yeoman's *Shield* and am not in communication with Elder Ephraim Jenson, I cannot vouch for his remarks, but feel safe in saying that if the whole report were published, his testimony would agree with that of Elder Whitaker as published in the Brooklyn *Citizen*.

[14] In quoting from "The Mysteries of Mormonism, by an Apostle's Wife," Mr. Evans reveals the character of his "dozens and dozens of witnesses." The reader will perceive that he depends largely on the most bitter anti-"Mormons" and apostates for his "evidence," but in quoting from "The Mysteries of Mormonism, by an Apostle's Wife," he certainly reaches the climax of this base testimony. This work was published in 1882, by Richard K. Fox, proprietor of the notorious *Police Gazette*. The author of these "Mysteries," undoubtedly a man, assumes the title of "An Apostle's Wife," in order to hide his perfidy. The work is one of the vilest and most contemptible of all anti-"Mormon" publications, and is most bitter in

One of the Mormon wives said that, and she ought to know whereof she affirms.

We have learned from the above statements that polygamy was not taught or practiced by Joseph Smith, but was introduced into an apostate branch of the church, after his death, as is admitted by Brigham Young and others of his followers.

Having read the works of the church for over a quarter of a century. I confidently affirm that there is not a single word, in a single sermon, lecture, statement, newspaper or church publication printed during the lifetime of the Prophet Joseph Smith wherever he, by word, has endorsed the doctrine of plurality of wives; not a single statement; and there is no Salt Lake Mormon breathing who can produce one and prove its authenticity.

But suppose you could prove that Joseph Smith secretly taught and practiced polygamy, that would not make it a Christian doctrine. If Joseph Smith secretly taught, practiced, or endorsed the doctrine of polygamy, he did it contrary to all the revelations given for the government of the church in the Bible, Book of Mormon, and Doctrine and Covenants; contrary to all his sermons, speeches, and public teachings; and he was a criminal before the law of his country, a base hypocrite before the God whom he openly worshiped, a despicable traitor to the woman whom he claimed to love and cherish as his wife, and was untrue to all the sacred principles of fidelity and integrity which he evinced in all his public utterances and conduct.

In the face of all this, the wife and children of Joseph Smith, together with thousands of people who knew him in life, refuse to believe the contradictory statements of Brigham Young and others who are wallowing in the mire of polygamy.

MY VISIT TO UTAH

If your father denies that he and I discussed the doctrine of polygamy, all I have to say about it is, that what he states is untrue. Here are a few points that may help him to remember what was said and done: When talking with Joseph F. Smith in Salt Lake City two years ago, he brought up a number of witnesses and I examined them—that is, he repeated the testimony of some who had testified. He finally said, "I can produce a living woman who will testify that Joseph Smith was a polygamist, and she knew it." I said, "Bring her along here and let us examine her." Well, I met "Aunt Lucy" Walker Kimball, to whom you refer, and we talked

---

its denunciation of the Prophet Joseph Smith. In it he is called a "lusty toper," "the worst of a bad breed," "an ignorant, brutal loafer," "immoral, false and fraudulent," and the author says, "*this* is the man who founded what he dared to call a faith, and grafted on the United States the religion of licentiousness and bodily lust known as Mormonism." An apology is perhaps due for even referring to this matter, but since Mr. Evans makes this work one of the chief of his "dozens and dozens of witnesses," I feel that he should be exposed. He professes to believe in the divine mission of Joseph Smith, and yet calls upon us to accept the wicked falsehoods of this disreputable witness, whom he declares *"ought to know whereof she affirms."* Shame upon the man who draws his inspiration from such a source!

the matter over, and here is the one point to which I want to draw your attention, to show how these poor dupes of Brigham Young may be led. Coming to the testimony of Emma Smith, I said, "You were personally acquainted with Emma Smith?" "Yes." "What have you to say as to her integrity, as to her fidelity and honor?" The old woman looked me fair in the face and said, "Emma Smith was one of God's noble women—she was truth personified; and anything that Emma Smith may say you can bank on it until the day of your death." "Well," I said, "she testifies that her husband never had any wife but her; she testifies that she never heard of that revelation on polygamy until you folks had gone to Salt Lake; she testifies she never saw it, and she testifies that it is an unmitigated falsehood manufactured by Brigham Young; that he stated that she had the revelation and burned it. Now what have you to say to that?" I said. She looked me fair in the face and said, "You can afford to build on anything that Emma Smith has to say." "Thank you," said I.

It is true that she told me she was married to Joseph Smith May 1, 1843; but when I showed her that the so-called revelation permitting a plurality of wives was dated July 12, 1843, and referred to her former testimony as given in the *Historical Record*, and that given under oath in the Temple Lot suit, she was confounded. I felt sorry for the old lady as she sat silent and confounded.

It is true that I saw a very old lady in your father's parlor, as she came slowly in for prayers. Your father said, "This is Catherine Phillips Smith. She was married to my father, Hyrum Smith, and she has never married since. I am not sure that the old lady heard a word. It is certain that *she did not testify to me*, but it was your father who made the statement, and at once called us to prayer, thus preventing me from speaking to the old lady.

Lorenzo Snow did testify to me, as stated; but then and there, in the presence of Joseph F. Smith and George Q. Cannon, I showed *his testimony to be false, by his own evidence*, when given *under oath*, and *by his sister's statement signed in 1842*. At this, Snow, Cannon and Smith were all much annoyed. So much for your father's statement, which says "you did not say one word to him in relation to polygamy."

YOUR FATHER'S FIRST WIFE

You seem to feel sore over the statement that your father's "first wife died broken hearted and insane"; and you add, "If you mean to insinuate that this condition, if true, was the result of any act whatever on the part of my father, it is also slanderously false." I insinuate nothing; let the public judge the facts. Your father's first wife was his cousin; she refused to consent to additional wives, and when he persisted in marrying the Lambson sisters, she obtained a divorce in California. Julina and Edna Lambson were sisters and were married to Joseph F. Smith on the same day.[15]

---

[15] This whole statement is absolutely false, and there was not the least shadow of reason for uttering it. President Smith's first wife did not refuse to consent to additional wives. He did not marry two sisters on the same day. In depending on the unreliable Alfred Henry Lewis for his argument, Mr. Evans shows the desperate weakness of his position. It would be a hard matter to squeeze more falsehoods in the space occupied by the article of A. H. Lewis, from which Mr. Evans quotes so faithfully.

Number of wives married to Joseph F. Smith since 1865: 6

Number of children born to him in 38 years: 42

Number of children born since plural marriage was prohibited in 1890: 13

Children of Julina Lambson Smith: 2

Children of Sarah Richards Smith: 2

Children of Edna Lambson Smith: 2

Children of Alice Kimball Smith: 3

Children of Mary Schwartz Smith: 4

Estimated income available for supporting five establishments: $75,000

Corporations, banks and factories of which Joseph F. Smith is a director: 20

The only Mormon Apostle who surpasses the record of President Smith is M. W. Merrill, with 8 wives, 45 children, and 156 grandchildren.—*Collier's* for March 26, 1894 (1904).

*   *   *   *   *

While in Utah I was informed that your father's first wife died broken hearted and insane. God and civilization know that a woman who loved her husband from youth up has enough to break her heart and send her insane when her husband will marry two other women, both sisters, in one day.

Perhaps you will be assisted to view the matter as I do, should you read the following in the Book of Mormon, Jacob 2:6, 7. Here it is stated, in consequence of polygamy, "ye have broken the hearts of your tender wives." Does this make the prophet an asperser or a scandalmonger?

I have answered your letter as it appeared in the Toronto *Star* as fully as space would permit.

Respectfully,
R. C. Evans.

Toronto, Ontario, March 1, 1905.[16]

---

[16] This letter is dated March 1, 1905, but was not written until sometime after April 19, 1905, for on the latter date Mr. Evans wrote: "You may look for reply to your letter as it appeared in the Toronto *Star*, as soon as I have time to reply thereto." This reply was received May 5, 1905.

A REJOINDER TO MR. R. C. EVANS' LETTER

Salt Lake City, May 23, 1905.

Mr. R. C. Evans,
Counselor in Presidency of Reorganized Church.

Sir:—Your reply to my open letter of February 17 was received May 5. Whether I was "fair, dispassionate and also candid" in my letter, or, as you seem to think, "guilty of a labored effort to cover up the true facts regarding 'blood atonement, polygamy, etc.'" and "your faith"—which was not discussed—I am perfectly willing to leave to the judgment of "those who read" the same in the Toronto *Star*. So on this point we may both rest satisfied.

BLOOD ATONEMENT

I will now consider your "labored effort to cover up the *true facts* regarding blood atonement."

In my letter I candidly placed the true belief and teachings of the Latter-day Saints in relation to this doctrine before you. This fact appears to be displeasing to you, as it overturns your conclusions and accusations against our people. If you desire to know the correct position of the Church on this doctrine, I would recommend a careful study of John Taylor's *Meditation and Atonement* and Charles W. Penrose's *Blood Atonement*, which was published in answer to such wicked misrepresentations as I claim you have made in relation to this principle and our belief in relation thereto. There is no reason for any person to misunderstand our position, unless he desires to do so. I claim, too, that we are in a better position to teach that which we believe than is the stranger who attempts to present our case, especially if he is antagonistic or unfriendly.

If you do not believe the doctrine of blood atonement as that doctrine is taught by the Church of Jesus Christ of Latter-day Saints, which church you are pleased to call "Utah Mormonism," then I say that you *do not* believe in the atonement of our Lord and Savior Jesus Christ. To this I will refer later.

You delight—as all anti-"Mormons" do—in referring to statements made by President Brigham Young, Jedediah M. Grant and others during the troublous times preceding the advent of Johnston's army into Utah. I see, too, that like many others, you place your own *desired* interpretation on their remarks, place them before the public in a garbled state, taking care to give the darkest interpretation possible from which the public may gather false conclusions. You take great pains to cover up the conditions prevailing which called forth such extreme and in some instances unwise remarks. Conditions in some respects akin to those surrounding the Saints in Missouri in 1838-39 when other unwise remarks were made by members of the leading quorums of the Church, but in a sense justifiable and which should be condoned under the trying circumstances that called them forth.[17]

THE CHURCH JUDGED FROM ITS ACCEPTED STANDARDS

Writing on this subject Elder B. H. Roberts, in his criticism on Harry Leon Wilson's plagarisms in his *Lions of the Lord*, declares the position taken by members of the Church and all fair-minded men in these words:

> "The justice of Burke's assertion has never been questioned, and without any wresting whatever it may be applied to "Mormon" leaders who sometimes spoke and acted under the recollection of rank injustice perpetrated against themselves and their people; or to rebuke rising evils against which their souls revolted."

Even the president of the Reorganized Church recognized this fact in his answer to *The American Baptist*, wherein he said:

> "Whoever counseled or did evil in those times (in Missouri) are responsible, personally, therefor; but the church, as such is no more responsible for it than were the early Christians for Peter's attempt to kill the high priest's servant when he cut off his ear with his sword. The church, as such, should be judged by its authorized doctrines and deeds, and not by the unauthorized sayings or doings of some or many of its members or ministers.
>
> It is not to be wondered at that in those times when the embryo authors and abettors of the "Border Ruffianism" that reigned in Missouri and Kansas from 1854 to 1865 had matters all their own

---

[17] I am not so blind in my admiration of the "Mormon" people or so bigoted in my devotion to the "Mormon" faith as to think there are no individuals in the Church chargeable with fanaticism, folly, intemperate speech, and wickedness; nor am I blind to the fact that some in their over-zeal have lacked judgment; and that in times of excitement, under stress of special provocation, even "Mormon" leaders have given utterances to ideas that are indefensible. But I have yet to learn that it is just in a writer of history, or of "purpose fiction," that "speak truly," to make a collection of these things and represent them as the essence of that faith against which said writer draws an indictment.

"No one would measure the belief of 'Christians,'" says a truly great writer, "by certain statements in the Fathers, nor judge the moral principles of Roman Catholics by prurient quotations from the Casuist; nor yet estimate Lutherans by the utterances and deeds of the early successors of Luther, nor Calvinists by the burning of Servetus. In all such cases the general standpoint of the times has to be first taken into account." — Edeshiem's Life and Times of Jesus the Messiah, preface p. 8.

A long time ago the great Edmund Burke in his defense of the rashness expressed in both speech and action of some of our patriots of the American revolution period said: "It is not fair to judge of the temper of the disposition of any man or any set of men when they are composed and at rest from their conduct or their expressions in a state of disturbance and irritation."

way, that some of the Saints, vexed, confused and excited, should have done many things unwisely and wrongfully, and contrary to the law of God." —*Saints' Herald*, 37:51.

With this I heartily agree.

Now, when the statements were made, which you in a garbled manner both quote and misquote, there was in Utah a class of individuals who spent the greater part of their time in circulating wicked and malicious reports about the Saints, threatening their lives, committing crimes and attempting to make the Saints their scape-goats. The officers of the law were General Government officials appointed by the President of the United States, and I am sorry to say, some of these were among the chief villifiers of the people. The most damnable and bloodthirsty falsehoods were concocted and served up to the people of the United States to stir them up to anger against the "despised Mormons." Almost every crime that was committed within a thousand miles of Salt Lake City was charged to the leaders of the "Mormon" people and became the foundation of a multitude of anti-"Mormon" publications that still flood the world. Because of these false and highly colored tales, in 1857—one year later than the time that most of the utterances were given on which you so delight to dwell—the Government of the United States sent an army to suppress in Utah a rebellion that never existed, and forced the Saints to defend themselves. When the Government found out how it had blundered it was humiliated.

Now, in brief, these were the conditions at the time, and is it any wonder that unwise and even harsh things were said? The wonder is that the people bore it as patiently as they did. The officers were non-"Mormons," the Territory was under Federal control and contained many Gentiles, many of whom were most bitter in their feelings and ever ready to accuse the Saints of crime. The government was strong enough to enforce the law if broken. Now, I ask you if you believe the horrors, as they have been pictured, could have existed under such conditions?

Such a state of affairs would have been a reproach and a shame to the American government. And no such state of affairs existed.

The conditions at the time led Jacob Forney, superintendent of Indian affairs in Utah, to declare in 1869:

> I fear, and I regret to say it, that with certain parties here there is a greater anxiety to connect Brigham Young and other Church dignitaries with every criminal offense than dilgent endeavor to punish the actual perpetrators of crime.
>
> Bancroft's History of Utah, p. 561.
> Whitney's History of Utah, p. 108, vol. 1.

Mr. Forney was a Gentile official and the truth of this statement can be relied upon.

This being the case, Brigham Young and the "Mormon" people could not have engaged in the crimes charged against them.

In connection with this let me quote from Bancroft:

It is not true that Mormons are not good citizens, lawabiding and patriotic. Even when hunted down, and robbed and butchered by the enemies to their faith, they have not retaliated. On this score they are naturally very sore. When deprived of those sacred rights given to them in common with all American citizens, when disfranchised, their homes broken up, their families scattered, their husband and father seized, fined and imprisoned, they have not defended themselves by violence but have left their cause to God and their country. — History of Utah, pp. 390-392.

Again, I repeat, that the presence in Utah of apostates and anti-"Mormons" from the beginning and "that there are men living in Utah today who left the Church in the earliest history of our State, who feel as secure and are just as secure and free from molestation from their former associates as you or any other man could be," proves the falseness of the malicious accusation that "Utah was for years a land of assassination and a field of blood."

MR. EVANS' FALSE QUOTATIONS

"What shall be done with the sheep that stink the flock so? We will take them, I was going to say, and cut off their tails two inches behind their ears; however I will use a milder term, and say cut off their ears."

Your conclusion is most certainly far fetched. Had you continued the quotation your attempt would have appeared even more ridiculous. The next sentence is:

"But instead of doing this, we will try to cleanse them; and will wash them with soap; that will come nigh taking off the skin; we will then apply a little Scotch snuff, and a little tobacco, and wash them again until we make them clean."

And you try to make this appear as threatening life! It is apparent that your sense of humor has been sadly neglected. This whole passage is humorous and you make yourself ridiculous by not having discovered it.

Again from Parley P. Pratt, you quote:

"My feelings are with those who have spoken, decidedly and firmly so."

This from page 84. Then you skip to page 86 and add:

"I need not repeat their doom, it has been told here today, they have been faithfully warned."

Then three paragraphs off, the following:

"It is too late in the day for us to stop and inquire whether such an outcast has the truth."

This method of proving things reminds me of the reason why you should be hanged:

And Judas "went out and hanged himself."

"Go thou and do likewise."

Now let me quote some extracts from this discourse which you purposely left out.

"Sooner than be subjected to a repetition of these wrongs, *I for one*, would rather march out today and be shot down. These are my feelings, and have been for some time. Talk about liberty of conscience! Have not men liberty of conscience here? Yes. The Presbyterian, Methodists, Quakers, etc., have *here* the liberty to worship God in their own way, and so has every man in the world. People have the privilege of apostatizing from this Church and worshiping devils, snakes, toads, or geese, if they please, and only let their neighbors alone. But they have not the privilege to disturb the peace, nor to endanger life or liberty; that is the idea. If they will take that privilege, *I need not repeat their doom, it has been told here today, they have been faithfully warned.*"

Again:

"He (Gladden Bishop) was disfellowshiped, and received on his professions of repentance, so often, that the Church at length refused to admit him any more as a member. These apostates talk of proof. Have we not proved Joseph Smith to be a prophet, a restorer, standing at the head of this dispensation? Have we not proved the priesthood which he placed upon others by the command of God?

"I see no ground, then, to prove or to investigate the calling of an apostate, who has always been trying to impose upon this people. *It is too late in the day for us to stop and inquire whether such an outcast has the truth.*

"We have truths already developed, unfulfilled by us—unacted upon. There are more truths poured out from the eternal fountain, already than our minds can contain, or that we have places or preparations to carry out. And yet we are called upon to prove—what? *Whether an egg that was known to be rotten fifteen years ago, has really improved by reason of age!*

"'*You are going to be destroyed,*' say they. '*Destruction awaits this city.*' Well! what if we are? We are as able to be destroyed as any people living. What care we whether we are destroyed or not? These old tabernacles will die of themselves, if left alone.

"We have nothing to fear on that head, for we are as well prepared to die as to live. One thing we have heard today, and I am glad to hear it. We shall not be destroyed in the old way—as we have been heretofore. We shall have a change in the manner, at least. We shall probably be destroyed *standing, this time,* and not in a *sitting*, or *lying position*. We can die as well as others who are not as well prepared! I am glad that while we do live we shall not submit to be yoked or saddled like a dumb ass. We shall not stand still to see men, women, and children murdered, robbed, plundered, and driven any more, as in the States heretofore. Nor does God require it at our hands. That is the best news we have heard today. * * *

"It is the policy not to wait till you are killed, but act on the defensive while you still live. I have said enough on this subject."—pp. 86-87.

The vicious malignancy of a depraved mind is made so apparent in this contrast between your garbled quotations and the whole truth, that it scarcely deserves further comment.

I have quoted quite extensively in order to show the reason for these remarks of which you quote such brief and disjointed extracts. You should remember that the Saints had but a short time before being driven from their homes at the cannon's mouth, and were forced to traverse a desert under the most trying circumstances to find a new abode where they could rest in peace and call their souls their own. When followed, as they were, by a miserable class that were determined to again have them driven, where heaven only knows, in their might and righteous indignation they firmly took their stand for home and liberty. I for one, say that they were justified in this course, the protection of their liberty, honor and lives. Had the threats of their enemies here in Utah been carried out as they boasted that they would be, and as they were carried out in Missouri and Illinois, then Brigham Young and his people would have been as thoroughly justified in unsheathing the bowie knife, to conquer or die, as were the patriots at Lexington and Bunker Hill!

Home and liberty and life, with the right to worship God, are just as dear to a "Mormon" as to members of any other denomination or even an apostate "Mormon," and when the "Mormons" are persecuted, driven and slain and forced to seek a home in the savage wilds, would any honest man blame them if they declined to move again?

Why is it worse for "Utah Mormons" to defend themselves than for "Mormons" at Crooked river and Nauvoo? Even the noble Prophet Joseph Smith, when dragged from home and persecuted by wicked men, solemnly demurred. Said he to the Saints at Nauvoo on the 30th day of June, 1843, after his escape from Missourian assassins:

"Before I will be dragged away again among my enemies for trial, *I will spill the last drop of blood in my veins and will see all my enemies in hell!* To bear it any longer would be a sin, and I will not bear it any longer. Shall we bear it any longer? (one universal, No! ran through all the vast assembly like a loud peal of thunder.) * * * If mobs come upon you any more here, dung your gardens with them. We don't want any excitement; but after we have done all, we will rise up Washington-like and break off the hellish yoke that oppresses us, and will not be mobbed!"

I have copied this from the manuscript history of the Prophet Joseph Smith, as it was recorded at the time. I have learned also that it is corroborated by the journal of Wilford Woodruff of the same date—June 30th, 1843.

UTAH NOT A FIELD OF BLOOD

You say, "I have read that which leads me to believe that under Brighamism"—as you slurringly remark—"Utah was for years a land of assassination and a field of blood," and then you ask me, "what of the Mountain Meadows massacre,—the destruction of the Aiken party; the dying confession of Bishop J. D. Lee; the Hickman butcheries; the Danties?"

Well, that which you have read counts for but little when the source is considered. Your case is most certainly desperate when you are forced to accept the statements of murderers.

It's a strange thing that you and many of your elders accept all the blood-curdling tales from Beadle, Stenhouse and other apostate sources *when* they happen to refer to Brigham Young and "Utah Mormons," and denounce the same sources when they refer to the Prophet Joseph Smith. Yet, I repeat, the same class of charges—in many respects identical—that you charge against Brigham Young, of murder, bloodshed, adultery, and even Danties, were first made by bitter enemies of the Church before the death of the Prophet Joseph Smith, and that just such falsehoods brought about the bitterness that resulted in his death.

You resort to sources that even the editor of your official paper denounces as "Idle and vicious stories gathered from the awful files of terrible tales told about the Mormons, by those at enmity with them."—*Saints Herald* 52:2.

If you desire to know the character of Christ do you accept the statements of the Roman guard at the sepulchre? the Jew with blood-stained hands who rejoices in his death? and the anti-Christian? Wherein then, is your consistency in asking me to accept the testimony of those whose hands are imbrued in blood, apostates and bitter enemies of my people?

Very well then, I return your question. What about them? Pray tell, what about the Mountain Meadows massacre? the Aiken party? the confessions of Lee? (by the way, the fact that you call him a "Bishop" proves the source of your information); what about Hickman and above all, the Danties?

When Alfred Henry Lewis, in *Collier's Weekly* of March 26, 1964, stated, "Brigham Young invented his destroying angels, placed himself at their head, and when a man rebelled had him murdered, if one fled the fold, he was pursued and slain," he repeated one of the most colossal falsehoods ever uttered. Nor is that the only falsehood in his article you are pleased to quote.

Brigham Young was *not* a man of blood. The "Mormon" people were *not* guilty of the Mountain Meadows massacre.[18] There was no destruction of an Aiken par-

---

[18] Writing of the Mormon Meadows massacre Hubert H. Bancroft, in his History of Utah, page 544 says: "Indeed it may well be understood at the outset that this horrible

ty. Hickman and Lee are not worth the mention; and the Danties! Had you not better read Church history of 1838? In Utah there never were destroying angels or Danties, except in the imagination of bitter anti-"Mormons" and I am satisfied that Mr. R. C. Evans knows that fact.

CHARACTER OF THE "MORMONS"

In answer to your many charges about Utah and the "Mormons," I desire to refer to credible references from witnesses who understood the truth and were bold enough to express it.

Last winter there was a census taken of the Utah Penitentiary and the Salt Lake City and county prisons with the following result:—In Salt Lake City there are about 75 Mormons to 25 non-Mormons; in Salt Lake County there are about 80 Mormons to 20 non-Mormons; yet in the city prison there were 29 convicts, all non-Mormons. In the county prison there were 6 convicts all non-Mormons. The jailer stated that the county convicts for the five years past were all anti-Mormons except *three!* * * *

Out of the 200 saloon, billiard, bowling alley and pool table keepers not over a dozen even profess to be Mormons. All of the bagnios and other disreputable concerns in the territory are run and sustained by non-Mormons. Ninety-eight per cent of the gamblers in Utah are of the same element. * * * Of the 250 towns and villages in Utah, over 200 have no "gaudy sepulchre of departed virtue," and these two hundred and odd towns are almost exclusively Mormon in population. Of the suicides committed in Utah ninety odd per cent are non-Mormons, and of the Utah homicides and infanticides over 80 per cent are perpetrated by the 17 per cent of "outsiders."—Phil Robinson, in *Sinners and Saints*, p. 72.

The Logan police force is a good-tempered looking young man. There is another to help him, but if they had not something else to do they would either have to keep arresting each other, in order to pass the time, or else combine to hunt gophers and chipmunks.—*Sinners and Saints*, p. 142.

Whence have the public derived their opinions about

crime, so often and so persistently charged upon the Mormon church and its leaders, was the crime of an individual, the crime of a fanatic of the worst stamp, one who was a member of the Mormon church, but of whose intentions the church knew nothing, and whose bloody acts the members of the church, high and low, regard with as much abhorrence as any out of the church. Indeed, the blow fell upon the brotherhood with threefold force and damage. There was the cruelty of it, which wrung their hearts; there was the odium attending its performance in their midst; and there was the strength it lent their enemies further to malign and molest them. The Mormons denounce the Mountain Meadows massacre, and every act connected therewith, as earnestly and as honestly as any in the outside world. This is abundantly proved, and may be accepted as a historical fact."

Mormonism? From *anti-Mormons* only. I have ransacked the literature of the subject, and yet I really could not tell any one where to go for an impartial book about Mormonism, later in date than Burton's "City of the Saints," published in 1862. * * * But put Burton on one side and I think I can defy any one to name another book about the Mormons worthy of honest respect. From that truly *awful* book, "The History of the Saints," published by one Bennet (even an anti-Mormon has styled him "the greatest rascal that ever came to the west") in 1842, down to Stenhouse's in 1873, there is not, to my knowledge a single Gentile work before the public that is not utterly unreliable from distortion of facts. Yet it is from these books—for there are no others—that the American public has acquired nearly all its ideas about the people of Utah.—*Sinners and Saints*, p. 245.

And in relation to opposing evidence, almost every book that has been put forth respecting the people of Utah by one not a Mormon, is full of calumny, each author apparently endeavoring to surpass his predecessor in the libertinism of abuse. Most of these are written in a sensational style, and for the purpose of deriving profit by pandering to a vitiated public taste, and are wholly unreliable as to facts.—*Bancroft's History of Utah*, preface page 7.

It is only fair to state that no Gentile, even the unprejudiced, who are rare aves, however long he may live or intimately he may be connected with Mormons, can expect to see anything but the superficies. * * *

The Mormons have been represented, and are generally believed to be, an intolerant race. I found the reverse far nearer the fact. The best proof of this is that there is hardly one anti-Mormon publication, however untruthful, violent, or scandalous, which I did not find in Great Salt Lake City.—Burton's *City of the Saints*, p. 203.

I have not yet heard the single charge against them as a community, against their habitual purity of life, their integrity of dealing, their toleration of religious differences in opinion, their regard for the laws, or their devotion to the Constitutional government under which we live, that I do not from my own observation, or the testimony of others know to be unfounded.—General Thomas L. Kane, U. S. A., *The Mormons*, p. 83.

The Mormons are sober, industrious and thrifty.—Bishop Spaulding, of the Episcopalian Church, in the *Forum*, March, 1887.

Had the Mormons been a low, corrupt or shiftless people they never would or could have done what they did in Utah. * * * When they controlled their own city of Salt Lake it contained no saloons, gambling houses or places of ill repute, and when the town had grown to be a goodly city order was kept by two constables. If by their fruits we may know them, the Mormons deserve our confidence and praise.—*The Brooklyn Eagle*, editorial of Aug. 12, 1897.

I shall not arraign the Mormon people as wanting in comparison with other people in religious devotion, virtue, honesty, sobriety, industry, and the graces and qualities that adorn, beautify and bless life.—Caleb W. West, Governor of Utah (and a strong anti-Mormon) in report to Secretary of the Interior for 1888.

I know the people of the east have judged the Mormons unjustly. They have many traits worthy of admiration. I know them to be honest, faithful, prayerful workers.—D. S. Tuttle, Bishop Episcopalian Church.

I never met a people so free from sensualism and immorality of every kind as the Mormons are. Their habits of life are a thousand per cent superior to those who denounce them so bitterly.—Mrs. Olive N. Robinson. (I recommend this to you.)

I assure you there are many others of equal force but this should be sufficient to prove the scandalous effusions false that you profess to believe true.

GAGGING AT A KNAT

I am glad you profess to believe the Bible. There is one other thing which appears strange to me, that is, why you are continually denouncing Brigham Young and "Utah Mormonism," and calling Utah a "land of assassination and a field of blood," because vile men without conscientious scruples have accused the people of many false and lurid tales of blood, and at the same time with sanctimonious countenance and upturned eyes you swallow the following without a gulp:

"Thus saith the Lord of hosts. * * * Now go up and smite Amalek, and utterly destroy all that they have, and spare them not; but slay both man and woman, infant and suckling, ox and sheep, camel and ass." I Samuel 15:3 (I. T.)

Haven't you swallowed the camel and gagged at his tail?

THE DOCTRINE OF BLOOD ATONEMENT

Just a word or two now, on the subject of blood atonement. *What is that doctrine?* Unadulterated if you please, laying aside the pernicious insinuations and lying charges that have so often been made. It is simply this: Through the atonement of Christ all mankind may be saved, by obedience to the laws and ordinances of the Gospel. This salvation is two-fold; General,—that which comes to all men irrespective of a belief in Christ—and Individual,—that which man merits through his own acts through life and by obedience to the laws and ordinances of the Gospel.

But man may commit certain grievous sins—according to his light and knowledge—that will place him beyond the reach of the atoning blood of Christ. If then he would be saved he must make sacrifice of his own life to atone—so far as in his power lies—for that sin, for the blood of Christ alone under certain circumstances will not avail.

Do you believe this doctrine? If not, then I do say you do not believe in the true doctrine of the atonement of Christ! This is the doctrine you are pleased to call the "blood atonement of *Brighamism*." This is the doctrine of Christ our *Redeemer*, who died for us. This is the doctrine of Joseph Smith, and I accept it.

In whose stead did Christ die? I wish your church members could be fair enough to discuss this subject on *its merits*.

I again recommend you to a careful reading of the quotations in my open letter. You will find them as follows: Book of Mormon,—II Nephi 9:35. Alma 1:13, 14, and 42:19. Bible,—Genesis 9:12, 13, (I. T.) Luke 11:50. Hebrews 9:22 and 10:26-29. I John 3:15 and 5:16. Doctrine and Covenants,—87:7. 101:80. 42:18, 19, 79. (Utah edition.)

To these I will add:

> "Whoso killeth any person, the murderer shall be put to death by the mouth of witnesses; but one witness shall not testify against any person to cause him to die.
>
> Moreover ye shall take no satisfaction for the life of a murderer, which is guilty of death; but he shall be surely put to death.
>
> So ye shall not pollute the land wherein ye are; for blood it defileth the land; and the land cannot be cleansed of the blood that is shed therein, but by the blood of him that shed it."—Numbers 35:30, 31, 33. (I. T.)[19]

Do you want a few references of where men were righteously slain to atone for their sins? What about the death of Nehor? (Alma 1:15) Zemnariah and his followers (III Nephi 4:27-28). What about Er and Onan, whom the Lord slew? (Gen. 38:7, 10), of Nadab and Abihu? (Lev. 10:2) and the death of Achan? (Joshua 7:25.)

Were not these righteously slain to atone for their sins? And it was of this class of cases that President Young referred in his discourse you misquote (*Journal of Discourses* 4:220). He tells us so, in the same discourse in the portion which you *did not quote*. It is:

"Now take the wicked, and I can refer you to where the Lord had to slay every soul of the Israelites that went out of Egypt except Caleb and Joshua. He slew them by the hand of their enemies, by the plague and by the sword. Why? Because he loved them and promised Abraham he would save them."

---

[19] See also Doctrine and Covenants section 101:80, on this point.

POLYGAMY

In using the term "polygamy" in reference to the principle that was taught and practiced by the Saints, I desire it distinctly understood that I use it in the sense of a man having more than one wife. Polygamy, in the sense of plurality of husbands and of wives never was practiced in the Church of Jesus Christ of Latter-day Saints in Utah or elsewhere; but Celestial marriage—including a plurality of wives—was introduced by the Prophet Joseph Smith and was practiced more generally by the saints under the administration of President Brigham Young.

You say that you have no evidence that those men, *viz.* Lyman Wight, James J. Strang, Gladden Bishop, William Smith and others that I mentioned to you "practiced *polygamy*" before plural marriage was "introduced" (as claimed by you) by Brigham Young. You said polygamy was "introduced" eight years after the Prophet's death by Brigham Young. If so, then why did these men practice it before that time? I was satisfied that you would not exert yourself in seeking for this knowledge and tried to help you find the information.

POLYGAMY IN THE "FACTIONS"

In a letter written by the President of the Reorganized church by Mr. Joseph Davis of Wales, dated Lamonia, Oct. 13, 1899, I read:

> "Nearly all the factions into which the church broke had plural marriage in some form. None in the form instituted by President Young. Sidney Rigdon had one form practiced by but a few, and that spasmodically, as an outburst of religious fervor rather than as a settled practice. William Smith had a sort of Priestess Lodge, in which it was alleged there was a manifestation of licentiousness. This he denied, and I never had actual proof of it. Gladden Bishop taught something like it, but I believe he was himself the only practioner. James J. Strang had a system something like Mohamet, four I think, being allowed the king. Lyman Wight had a system but it had no very extended range. President Young's system you may know of."

It is true that William Smith denied that he taught "polygamy" but that he practiced plural marriage he cannot deny. Jason W. Briggs said he (William) did, and that is why Mr. Briggs left his church. Plaintiff's Abstract, Temple Lot suit, p. 395. Hist. of Reorg. Ch. vol. 3:200 and *The Messenger*, vol. 2. William entered into plural marriage in the Prophet's day and his wives lived here in Utah. They are Precilla M. Smith, Sarah Libby and Hannah Libby. One of these is still living.

The third volume of your church history says of Lyman Wight:

> "Lyman Wight lived and died an honorable man, respected well by those who knew him best. The only thing that can be urged against his character is that about 1845 or 1846 he entered into the practice of polygamy, but we have seen no record of any teaching of his upon the subject."

The fact is that Lyman Wight entered into that relation before the time here mentioned. Affidavits in this regard can be produced but it will be unnecessary.

That John E. Page practiced "polygamy" I have the testimony of his wife, Mrs. Mary Eaton of Independence, who told me and others, in August 1904, that she *gave her husband*, John E. Page, other wives.

These men did not follow Brigham Young, but denounced him, yet they practiced plural marriage and did not get that doctrine from him.

THE TESTIMONY OF A BOGUS WIFE

The "testimony" you submit from President Young's "legal wife" is spurious. It matters not if you did receive the "information" from your uncle. The poor man was tricked and deceived. Bogus "wives" and "daughters" of President Young have "worked" the public before. Mary Ann Angel Young, President Young's legal wife, was not in Colorado in 1860 and 1861. She never was divorced and died in this city true to her husband, his family and the faith, on the 27th day of June, 1882. (*News*, July 5, 1882.) So much for this "bogus" testimony.

TESTIMONY IMPEACHED

The testimony of T. B. H. and Fanny Stenhouse is sufficiently impeached in the *Saints' Herald*, vol. 52, p. 2; 20, p. 602, and *Sinners and Saints*, p. 245. The woman's bitterness would condemn her writings. However I will mention one statement—you make Mrs. Stenhouse say: "It is reported by Fanny Stenhouse and many others, that Joseph Smith said, 'If ever the Church had the misfortune to be led by Bro. Brigham, he would lead it to hell.'" She gives this as a rumor that is "reported," so do the "many others" who are mostly from your church. Oh, yes, I have heard of this before. But do you know where the report originated? It originated with the apostate and would-be assassin, Robert D. Foster, who threatened the Prophet Joseph's life in 1844, and who was one of the incorporators and advocates of the notorious *Nauvoo Expositor*, and one of the chief actors in bringing about the martyrdom, June 27, 1844. In a toadying letter to your president, dated February 14, 1874, he said the prophet "remarked, in the presence of Mr. Law, Bishop Knight, John P. Greene, Reynolds Cahoon, and some others, that if ever Brigham Young became the leader of the Church, he would lead them down to hell."

MARVELOUS GROWTH OF THE CHURCH

I decline to accept the statements of such a character; besides, President Young did not lead the Church to hell, but preserved it, and under his direction it grew, expanded, and accomplished a wonderful, even a miraculous work. In the reclamation of the arid west, the permanent establishment of prosperous communities in the desert wilds, and for their unity, strength, and industrial and temporal independence, the "Mormon" people are today the marvel, if not the admiration of the thinking world. They came here with nothing but the good will of God. They began in poverty, and "having almost nothing to invest," says Mr. William E. Symthe in *The Conquest of Arid America*, "except the labor of their hands and brains, and that all they have expended in a period of fifty years for all classes of improvements—from the first shanty to the last turret of the last temple—came primarily from the soil."

Again he says in the same work:

TESTIMONY OF MR. SMYTHE

Nowhere else has the common prosperity been reared upon firmer foundations. Nowhere else are institutions more firmly buttressed or better capable of resisting violent economic revolutions. The thunder cloud that passed over the land in 1893, leaving a path of commercial ruin from the Atlantic to the Pacific, was powerless to close the door of a single Mormon store, factory or bank. Strong in prosperity, the co-operative industrial and commercial system stood immovable in the hour of widespread disaster. The solvency of these industries is scarcely more striking than the solvency of the farmers from whom they draw their strength. No other governor, either in the West or in the East, is able to say what the Honorable Heber M. Wells said in assuming the chief magistracy of the new state in January, 1896, "We have in Utah," said the young governor. "19,816 farms, and 17,584 of them are absolutely free from incumbrance." A higher percentage in school attendance and lower percentage of illiterates than even in the State of Massachusetts, is another of Utah's proud records. P. 71.

THE GUIDANCE OF JEHOVAH

Without the divine guidance and the constant watchcare of Jehovah over the destinies of the "Mormon" pioneers, with Brigham Young at their head, the West today would be but a barren wilderness. Under the leadership of Brigham Young the "Mormon" people prospered, and he left them in a better condition temporally and physically, and spiritually more united and more firmly established in the faith than they ever were before. Where among the so-called "factions" can you point to one that has accomplished the hundredth part of what the followers of Brigham Young have accomplished? They have all practically disappeared but one—gone to their destruction. And the one that remains will dissolve and disappear as surely as the sun shines. You cannot fight the work of God and prosper.

WILLIAM MARKS

The testimony of William Marks—a man who was out of harmony with the Prophet before the latter's death! This testimony of William Marks sounds too suspicious, given as it was, when it was, and describing an alleged conversation which never could have taken place. "The reader will please notice," said David Whitmer in his *Address* (p. 41), "this fact in regard to William Marks' statement; and that is, the time when Brother Joseph told him that polygamy must be put down in the Church." That time was a "few days" before the Prophet's death.

True, the Prophet was no "fool" (*Herald* 51:74), and such a "conversation" as this related by William Marks would have stamped him "foolish, irrational and a moral suicide," *because* he could not bring a charge against others for that for which he was himself responsible. The Prophet had plural wives, and had officiated in the ceremony of the sealing of plural wives to others. I have conversed with the principals in these cases, and know that they told the truth. Furthermore, Mr. Marks' testimony condemns itself. He proves—if he proves anything at all—that the Prophet was responsible for this doctrine. This thought is in harmony with the early teachings of the original elders of the Reorganization, for the time was when even your elders acknowledged that the Prophet received the revelation on celestial (including plural) marriage. On this point David Whitmer says:

> As time rolled on, many of the Reorganization saw that to *continue* to acknowledge that Brother Joseph received the revelation would bring bitter persecution upon themselves, as the public feeling at that time was very bitter. * * * The leaders of the Reorganized church, after a time, began to suppress their opinions concerning this matter. They would answer the question when asked about it *"I do not know whether Joseph Smith received the revelation or not."*

THE "SAINTS' HERALD" A WITNESS OF "POLYGAMY"

Now, if it is true—and I claim it is—that the leaders of the Reorganized church acknowledged that the Prophet received the revelation and practiced that principle, there must be some proof. Turn to the first volume of the *True L.D.S. Herald* and read the editorial on pages 6 to 11. It is on polygamy. After trying to explain the reason why the Prophet taught and practiced this doctrine, the editor said:

> And if the prophet be deceived when he hath spoken a thing, I, the Lord, have deceived the prophet, and I will stretch out my hand upon him and will destroy him from the midst of my people Israel. * * * We have here the facts as they have transpired and as they will continue to transpire in relation to this subject. The death of the prophet is one fact that has been realized, although he abhorred and repented of this iniquity before his death. Page 9.

And on page 27:

> He (Joseph Smith) caused the Revelation to be burned, and when he voluntarily came to Nauvoo and resigned himself into the arms of his enemies, he said that he was going to Carthage to die. At that time he also said that if it had not been for that accursed spiritual wife doctrine, he would not have come to that. By his conduct at that time he proved the sincerity of his repentance, and of his profession as a prophet. If Abraham[20] and Jacob, by repentance, can obtain salvation and exaltation, so can

----

[20] A polygamist the friend of God, whose praise you sing, and the man you are *glad* to call the father of the faithful.—*Saints' Herald* 52:437.

Joseph Smith.

Mark you, we have the evidence of the revelation from your own side and you well remember that but *one* could and did receive revelations. I do not accept the apology of your editor; I do not believe that the Prophet had the revelation burned, or called the doctrine accursed. My faith in Joseph Smith is such that if he had the revelation—which your witnesses declare he did—that it was from God as much as any other revelation he received!

TESTIMONY OF JASON BRIGGS

Jason W. Briggs, one of the founders of your church, in the Temple Lot suit, said:

> I heard something about a revelation on polygamy, or plural marriage, when I was in Nauvoo, in 1842. I heard there was one: there was talk going on about it at that time, and continued to be; but it was not called plural marriage; it was called sealing.

> You ask me what I understood this sealing to be, at the time the talk was going on. What I understood it to be was sealing a woman to a man to be his wife, to be his wife hereafter, his wife in the spirit world.

> I was asked in my direct examination if I did not hear of the doctrine of polygamy, etc., and I answered that I talked with members with reference to sealing, and I understood that the doctrine of sealing, was for eternity; it was sealing a man's wife to him for eternity, or wives, either. Record pp. 349, 431, 505.

TESTIMONY OF JAMES WHITEHEAD

James Whitehead said:

> There was an ordinance in the Church for sealing, as early as 1842 or 1843.

> They would be married according to the law of God, not only for time but for eternity as well.

These men were among the founders of your church.

SIDNEY RIGDON'S TESTIMONY

Sidney Rigdon, in a lengthy letter to his official paper, *The Messenger and Advocate*, in 1845 declared that the Prophet was responsible for the plural marriage doctrine, and said:

> This system was introduced by the Smiths some time before their death, and was the thing which put them in the power of their enemies, and was the immediate cause of their death. P. 475, vol. 2.

He says he "warned Joseph Smith and his family," and told them that destruction would come upon them if they continued in their course.

ORIGINAL RECORDS OF PLURALITY OF WIVES

You "confidently affirm that there is not a single word in a single sermon, lecture, statement, newspaper or Church publication *printed* during the life of Joseph Smith, wherein he by word has endorsed the doctrine of plurality of wives, not a single statement." Whether any such statement was ever *printed* in his lifetime or not I am not prepared to say. But I do know of such evidence being recorded during his lifetime, for I have seen it.

I have copied the following from the Prophet's manuscript record of Oct. 5, 1843, and know it is genuine:

> "Gave instructions to try those persons who were preaching, teaching or practicing the doctrine of plurality of wives; for according to the law, I hold the keys of this power in the last days; for there is never but one on earth at a time on whom this power and its keys are conferred; and I have constantly said no man shall have but one wife at a time unless the Lord directs otherwise."

There is also at the Historian's office in this city, a Bible, which I have before me, containing the record of the marriage of Melissa Lott to the Prophet Joseph Smith, which was recorded at the time, September 20, 1843. This Bible also contains the record of the sealing of Cornelius P. and Parmelia Lott, parents of Melissa, which was done by Patriarch Hyrum Smith in the Prophet's presence and with his "seal" or sanction. The president of your church has seen this record, and it matters not what he may say *now* he *then* acknowledged the genuineness of the record.

The following is also copied from the journal of William Clayton which is in the Historian's office:

> May 1st, (1843) A.M. At the Temple. At 10 married Joseph to Lucy Walker. P.M. at Prest. Joseph's; he has gone out with Woodsworth.

This is the same William Clayton who wrote the revelation at the direction and from the dictation of the Prophet July 12, 1843. However, this principle was first revealed to the Prophet several years before that time, as you learned in your conversation with President Lorenzo Snow, when you were in his office.

MORE EVIDENCE CONSIDERED

Right here we will consider the "evidence" you produce to show that "Joseph Smith and the Church during his lifetime condemned polygamy in the strongest terms." The testimony of the thirty-one witnesses you "produce" was against the "secret wife system" of the vile John C. Bennett who was excommunicated for betraying female virtue. This Bennett system had nothing to do with the system of celestial marriage introduced by the Prophet Joseph Smith, and was no more like the Prophet's doctrine than darkness is like daylight. The certificate of these parties that you mention was given in October 1842 (T. & S. 3:939), nearly one year before the revelation on celestial marriage was recorded. At that time the law of marriage in the Church was that adopted in 1835, and was binding on all who had accepted the higher law, and they were few in number.[21] The best proof that these "witnesses" did not condemn the celestial marriage doctrine of the prophet in this communication, is that out of the thirty-one, at least sixteen have testified that the Prophet introduced that system. One of this number of witnesses became the Prophet's wife, one performed a marriage ceremony in which the Prophet was married to a plural wife, and one other was a witness to such a marriage ceremony. At least six testify that the Prophet taught them the principle of plural marriage and the others, so far as I know, are not on record. That these witnesses were the dupes of Brigham Young cannot truthfully be said, for three of them left the Church and never followed Brigham Young, yet they testify of these things.

The action of Joseph and Hyrum Smith, as recorded in the *Times and Seasons* (5:3), wherein Hyrum Brown was cut off the Church for preaching polygamy and other false doctrines, was just and timely. The same action would have been taken at any other period of the existence of the Church. Polygamy never was a doctrine of the Church, and the system introduced by the Prophet Joseph Smith was not called by that name in his day. Nor was the system of the Prophet the same as that of Hyrum Brown; and if it had been, the ruling of the Prophet of October 5, 1843, would have cost Brown his standing in the Church, the polygamy of Brown and John C. Bennett was of their own make. In relation to this subject, I will quote from the *Life of John Taylor*, pages 223-224:

> The polygamy and gross sensuality charged by Bennett and repeated by those ministers in France, had no resemblance to celestial or patriarchal marriage which Elder Taylor knew existed at Nauvoo, and which he had obeyed. Hence in denying the false charges of Bennett, he did not deny the existence of that system of marriage that God had revealed; no more than a man would be guilty of denying the legal, genuine currency of the country by denying the genuineness and denouncing what he knew to be a mere counterfeit of it.

> Another illustration: Jesus took Peter, James and John into the mountain, and there met with Moses and Elias, and the glory of God shone about them, and these two angels talked with Jesus, and the voice of God was heard proclaiming Him to be the Son of God. After the glorious vision, as Jesus and His companions were descending the mountain, the former said: "Tell the vision to no man, until the Son of Man be risen from the dead." Suppose one

[21] Those thirty-one witnesses were: S. Bennett, George Miller, Alpheus Cutler, Reynolds Cahoon, Wilson Law, Wilford Woodruff, Newel K. Whitney, Albert Petty, Elias Higbee, John Taylor, Ebenezer Robinson, Aaron Johnson, Emma Smith, Elizabeth A. Whitney, Sarah M. Cleveland, Eliza R. Snow, Mary C. Miller, Lois Cutler, Thirza Cahoon, Ann Hunter, Jane Law, Sophia Marks, Polly Z. Johnson, Abagail Works, Catharine Petty, Sarah Higbee, Phebe Woodruff, Leonora Taylor, Sarah Hillman, Rosanna Marks, and Angeline Robinson.

of these apostles had turned from the truth before the Son of Man was risen from the dead and under the influence of wicked, lying spirit, should charge that Jesus and some of his favorite apostles went up into a mountain, and there met Moses and Elias,—or some persons pretending to represent them—together with a group of voluptuos courtesans, with whom they spent the day in licentious pleasure. If the other apostles denounced that as an infamous falsehood, would they be untruthful? No; they would not. Or would they be under any obligations when denying the falsehoods of the apostate to break the commandments the Lord had given them by relating just what had happened in the mountain? No; it would have been a breach of the Master's strict commandment for them to do that. So with Elder Taylor. While he was perfectly right and truthful in denying the infamous charges repeated by his oponents, he was under no obligation and had no right to announce to the world, at that time the doctrine of celestial marriage. It was not the law of the Church, or even the law of the Priesthood of the Church; the body thereof at the time knew little or nothing of it, though it had been revealed to the Prophet and made known to some of his most trusted followers. But today, now that the revelation on celestial marriage is published to the world, if the slanderous charges contained in the writings of John C. Bennett should be repeated, every Elder in the Church could truthfully and consistently do just what Elder Taylor did in France—he could deny their existence."

THAT UTAH VISIT

After receiving your letter, I requested of my father that he give me a written statement in answer to your charge that he "discussed" the doctrine of "polygamy" with you, and received the following:

Joseph F. Smith, Jr.

Dear Son:—You have submitted to me some statements made by Mr. R. C. Evans of the Reorganized church, and desire to know what I have to say about them. He says: "If your father denies that he and I discussed the doctrine of polygamy, all I have to say about it is, that what he states is untrue." Perhaps I could dismiss this statement precisely in the same way he has. I could certainly do so far more truthfully. He and I did not discuss the doctrine of "polygamy" at all. It is true I did introduce him to President Lorenzo Snow, to Aunt Lucy W. Smith, to Aunt Catherine P. Smith, to Heber J. Grant and a few others. Whatever "discussion" he had on the "doctrine of polygamy" may have been with these parties, but not with me. While in my company he was my guest by introduction from my cousin Joseph Smith, president of the Reorganized church, and I carefully avoided any discussion with him upon any and all differences of opinion which existed between us, the discussion of which could only have resulted in ill feeling and perhaps extreme bitterness. I treated him as any gentleman should treat another, not as an antagonist but as a stranger within my gates, indeed, as my guest; and when we parted it was with mutual good feelings and interchange of kindly wishes, without the slightest breath or suspicion of unpleasantness, which must have existed had we indulged in a "discussion of the doctrine of polygamy," or any other points of difference.

Aunt Catherine P. Smith was making us a short visit at the time, and I introduced her to Mr. Evans as the wife of my father, Hyrum Smith. They had some conversation, in which I took no part, and to the best of my recollection he drew out from her the fact that she was married to Hyrum Smith, by Joseph Smith the Prophet, in August 1843, in the brick office of Hyrum Smith, at Nauvoo, in the presence of her mother, Sarah Godshall Phillips, Mrs. Julia Stone and her daughter Hettie.

Mr. Evans attempted to cross-question her on her statement, but she stoutly and unequivocally affirmed the truth of what she had said. Mrs. Lizzie Wilcox, your mother and two or three other members of the family were present and heard what was said.

With reference to Mr. Evans' alleged interview with Aunt Lucy W. Smith at the Theatre, I need only say I occupied a seat adjoining them, and heard the conversation between them, and I have not the slightest recollection of the statement he has made about that interview. The strong point which he attempts to make is the fact that Lucy was married to the Prophet Joseph Smith, on May 1, 1843, while the revelation on plural marriage was dated "July 12, 1843," and her consequent embarrassment, was far-fetched; for no one knew better than she did that the revelation was given as far back as 1834, and was first reduced to writing in 1843. And on one could have been better prepared to state that fact than Aunt Lucy W. Smith. There could not be, therefore, any cause for embarrassment on her part on that score, and I apprehend she would have been one of the last persons to "sit silent and confused" under such an implied impeachment.

That she bore testimony to the good character of Aunt Emma Smith with reference to other matters than plural marriage is true; but not to her conduct toward that principle. Aunt Lucy is still living, and sound mentally and physically. She can, and no doubt will, fully clear away any sophistry and falsehood of Mr. Evans' statement of the alleged interview.

Referring to the interview with President Snow, Mr. Evans says: "Lorenzo Snow did testify to me as stated. But then and there, in the presence of Joseph F. Smith and George Q. Cannon, I showed his testimony to be false by his own evidence when given under oath, and his sister's statement signed in 1842. At this, Snow, Cannon and Smith were much annoyed. So much for your father's statement, which says 'you did not say one word to him in relation to polygamy.'" The fact is, President Snow gave Mr. Evans, in my presence and hearing, a plain, simple narration of the instructions he received from Joseph Smith in regard to the doctrine of plural marriage, including almost word for word the statement he had previously made under oath, and testified that Joseph informed him that his sister Eliza R. Snow had been sealed to him as his wife. This much and more in this line I distinctly heard and as distinctly remember, but I did not hear the alleged arraignment of President Snow's testimony by Mr. Evans, nor did I witness or experience any "annoyance" on the part of myself or anyone present because of the said arraignment. Indeed, I am prepared to affirm that Mr. Evans did not "then and there" in my presence and that of Geo. Q. Cannon, nor in the presence of any one there, "show his (Snow's) testimony to be false," either "by his own evidence when given under oath," or "by his sister's statement signed in 1842," or at any other time.

I am here constrained to say that Mr. Evans was treated by President Snow, as also by President George Q. Cannon and myself, in the most courteous and respectful manner, and so far as I observed his demeanor towards us was reciprocal and gentlemanly—and not one word was said to him by anyone nor by him to anyone in my presence that was in any degree discourteous, contentious or embarrassing.

I conclude, therefore, that the foregoing statements made by Mr. Evans, were after thoughts uttered by him with a view to misrepresent the truth and the facts, on the lines of the bitter and relentless opposition of himself and associates to the Church of Jesus Christ of Latter-day Saints in general, and the doctrine of plural marriage in particular, as revealed, taught and practiced by Joseph Smith himself, from whom Brigham Young and many others received it. On these matters they are so surcharged with animus that they will not receive, admit, or tell the truth.

With reference to Mr. Evans' allusion to my first wife I will simply say: She was most intimately acquainted from her childhood with the young lady who became my second wife, and it was with their full knowledge and consent that I entered into plural marriage, my first wife being present as a witness when I took my second wife, and freely gave her consent thereto. Our associations as a family were pleasant and harmonious.

It was not until long after the second marriage that my

first wife was drawn away from us, not on account of domestic troubles, but for other causes which I do not care to mention. In eight years of wedded life we had no children. She constantly complained of ill health and was as constantly under a doctor's care. She concluded to go to California for her health and before going procured a separation. This all occurred previous to 1867. On March 1, 1868 I married Sarah E. Richards, and January 1, 1870, I married Edna Lambson, from one to three years after my first wife separated from me, and had become a resident of California. She subsequently returned to Utah and later went to St. Louis where she died.

Your self-exaltation in classing yourself with Jacob is most stupendous, to say the least. He was above accepting idle rumors, from such sources as those given by the writer of the article of *Collier's* which you quote, and which are false. Jacob was no aspersor.

Aunt Catherine Phillips Smith also declares that she did testify to you in regard to her marriage and that you questioned her quite closely. My mother declares the same for she was present at the conversation. Presidents Snow and Cannon are not here to speak in their defense, but I am satisfied that they would bear witness to the foregoing letter. Aunt Lucy may testify for herself.

TESTIMONY OF LUCY W. SMITH

The day I received a copy of the *Ensign* containing your discourse from which you give extracts in your "reply," in relation to your "conversation" with Aunt Lucy W. Smith, I sent her a copy of your remarks with the request that she tell me if you had correctly reported her testimony. In the course of a few days I received this:

My Dear Boy: I very much regret not feeling able to answer your request at an earlier date. I am, however, much improved in health since coming to Logan, and take pleasure in declaring to you that the infamous discourse delivered 16th Feb. 1905 (the date of the *Ensign*) at St. Louis, Missouri, by Mr. Evans, is a fabrication of falsehoods and misrepresentations. I confess that I was not only surprised, but shocked beyond measure. Now one of the presidency of the Reorganized church, just think of it! And at the time he came to Salt Lake City three years ago, he claimed to be one of "young Joseph's apostles; came with a letter of introduction from cousin Joseph to his cousin Joseph F., saying that any courtesy shown him would be appreciated. Accordingly, Mr. Evans was shown every consideration. He accepted the generous hospitality of our President and his model family. Having expressed a desire to meet Mrs. Lucy W. Kimball, who was engaged that afternoon, arrangements were made to meet at the theatre, as he had to leave next day. He asked me many questions which I answered frankly—some very offensive hearsay questions that aroused my indignation, but I bore the ordeal as a martyr should. And from this opportunity sprang the wonderful discourse of wicked falsehood and malicious misrepresentation. O, shame! Where canst thou hide thy brazen face! How dare he resort to such infamy unless to satiate a morbid desire for notoriety among sensation-mongers, who seek not for light or truth! If so he only gratified the cravings of the basest and lowest caste.

I cannot believe that the once highly and beloved Emma who was so loyal and true to her husband in all the early trials and hardships to which he was subject, when in chains and bondage, when he was dragged from his bed, tarred and feathered, imprisoned and mocked and scoffed at, ridiculed and abused, and his life threatened by infuriated mobs and she stood by him and comforted him in all of his afflictions—I cannot believe after enduring all this for his sake, that Emma Smith ever denied seeing the revelation on celestial marriage after receiving it in good faith and accepting it as a command from God, *knowing* as I do, that she taught it to Eliza and Emily Partridge, Maria and Sarah Lawrence, and urged them to accept it by being sealed to her husband. She treated them kindly and considerately and knew they were associated with him as his wives. She was then a happy woman, until the tempter came in human form, and she partook of the apostate spirit so rife in those days. She could not deny these facts without sinning against her husband, sinning against his wives, against the truth, and against her God!

If her son insists that this denial was her last testimony he fastens a stigma on her once noble character in the estimation of her former friends and associates, who were familiar with the facts of the period referred to. This misguided son, young and without experience, was surrounded by his father's most wicked enemies who had betrayed his father, and had been instrumental in taking his life; and who, after they had accomplished this foul act, through sinister policies, determined to destroy the work his father was commanded to do, and had laid a permanent foundation on which to build up his church—the Church of Christ. They sought to influence his son against the teachings of his father, call him forth as a "leader" with promises of success, and good backing. Poor boy was flattered and led on and on, by crafty men, until he became an unbeliever of the principles his father had taught; and I cannot but believe that through such influences his mother has been misrepresented. I am unwilling to believe otherwise.

I expressed regrets to Mr. Evans in relation to the course taken by "young Joseph" through the influence of the bitter opponents of his father. I said he had closed his eyes to anything that would cast a ray of light on the vexed question: "Did my father have more [other] wives than my mother?" I answered truthfully without hesitation. Afterwards he went to Lehi, called on Melissa Lott, with whom he had been associated from early childhood and asked: "Will you answer me one question, I come to you knowing you will tell me the truth, were you my father's wife?" "Yes, Joseph, I was." "Where is your proof?" She stepped to the stand and took the family Bible opened to the family record, placed it on his knee and asked: "Do you recognize the handwriting?" "Certainly that is your father's (Cornelius P. Lott's) handwriting, know it as well as my own." Then read the marriage certificate of the Prophet Joseph and Melissa Lott.

Oliver Huntington who is still living testifies that they were very intimate as boys, and when together had often talked the matter over.

Referring to Mr. Evans again. I said: "Does this prove him (Joseph) an honest man?" Now does this cover the ground of your inquiry? I have so often been interrupted by callers, that I may not have been explicit enough. My personal testimony you already have, if not you can get it by referring to "Reminiscences of Latter-day Saints," by L. O. Littlefield, which you will find at the President's (Historian's) office.

Does this read much like she had been correctly represented?

BRIGHAM YOUNG UPHELD BY THE LORD

In reference to the wicked charge you make in your discourse mentioned in Aunt Lucy's letter, against President Young of practicing gross immorality while on his mission in England in 1840 and winter of 1841, a sufficient answer will be found in the revelation of January 19, 1841, wherein the Lord, by revelation through the Prophet Joseph Smith declares:

I give to you *my servant* Brigham Young, to be a President over the Twelve traveling Council,

Which Twelve hold the keys to open up the authority of my kingdom upon the four corners of the earth, and after that to send my word to every creature.

And the revelation of July 9, 1841, given after his return from England:

* * * Verily thus saith the Lord unto you, my servant Brigham, it is no more required at your hand to leave your family as in times past, for your offering is acceptable to me.

In this abusive charge against President Young you are striking at Jehovah, and accusing Him, either of condoning such a grievous sin, or failing to discover it. Such a charge as that is ridiculously absurd, I feel safe in accepting the word of the Lord in preference to the ribald, indecent statements of those who speak forth the vulgar desires of their own minds.

Respectfully,
Joseph F. Smith, Jr.

THE SAINTS' HERALD ON THE ORIGIN OF PLURAL MARRIAGE

In both replies to Mr. Evans, mention is made of two articles in the *Saints' Herald*, volume one, that were written by Isaac Sheen, the first editor of that paper. These references were ignored by Mr. Evans in his publication of a portion of the foregoing correspondence. It would occupy too much space to copy these articles in full as they are quite lengthy, but I feel that the gist of the matter should be presented in more detail than it is given in the replies.

Mr. Sheen's argument is that the Saints at Nauvoo "set up their idols in their heart," and went to the Prophet Joseph Smith and asked him to inquire of the Lord and ascertain from Him if it would not be proper for them to practice plural marriage. This the Prophet Joseph did and in answer the Lord gave him the revelation on celestial marriage, granting the practice of plural marriage, and then, after giving this revelation the Lord smote the Prophet for his 'iniquity' in asking for the revelation, and poured out wrath and indignation upon the Saints for their participation in what he calls "abominations."

Reference is also made to the prophecies of Ezekiel, Balaam and Micaiah to substantiate his theory which Mr. Sheen admits he is unable to "satisfactorily explain." An extensive quotation from the first article follows, which will give an idea of the position in which the members of the Reorganized church regard the Prophet Joseph Smith and the culmination of his most glorious mission.

STATEMENT OF ISAAC SHEEN

We might call your attention to many prophecies in the Bible which these backsliders[22] have fulfilled by their abominations. Ezekiel appears to have had a very clear manifestation of the wickedness of these men and the plan pursued by them, by which they embark into polygamy. In Ezekiel 14 c. 1, 5, v, the prophet says, "Then came certain elders of Israel unto me, saying, Son of man, these men have set up their idols in their heart and put the stumblingblock of their iniquity before their face: should I be inquired of at all by them? Therefore speak unto them, and say unto them, Thus saith the Lord God; Every man of the house of Israel that setteth up his idols in his heart, and putteth the stumblingblock of his iniquity before his face, and cometh to the prophet; I the Lord, will answer him that cometh according to the

[22] The Prophet Joseph Smith, Brigham Young and the Saints.

multitude of his idols; that I may take the house of Israel in their own heart, because they are all estranged from me through their idols." We have shown you that God gave a revelation unto us in which he commanded that every man should "cleave unto his wife and none else," and that he commanded us saying, "Repent and remember the Book of Mormon and the former commandments which I have given them, not only to say, but to do according to that which I have written," and that in that book there is much testimony against polygamy. All these instructions were sufficient for our guidance, but "men have set up their idols in their hearts, and put the stumblingblock of their iniquity before their faces." This adulterous spirit had captivated their hearts and they desired a license from God to lead away captive the fair daughters of His people, and in this state of mind they came to the Prophet Joseph. Could the Lord do anything more or less than what Ezekiel hath prophesied? The Lord hath declared by Ezekiel what kind of an answer he would give them, therefore he answered them according to the multitude of their idols. Paul had also prophesied that "for this cause God shall send them strong delusion, that they should believe a lie; that they all might be damned who believed not the truth, but had pleasure in unrighteousness." Both these prophecies agree. In Ezekiel's prophecy the Lord also says, "I will set my face against that man, and will make him a sign and a proverb, and I will cut him off from the midst of my people; and ye shall know that I am the Lord. And if the prophet be deceived when he hath spoken a thing, I the Lord have deceived that prophet,[23] and I will stretch out my hand upon him and I will destroy him from the midst of my people Israel. And they shall bear the punishment of their iniquity; the punishment of the prophet shall be even as the punishment of him that seeketh unto him; that the house of Israel may go no more astray from me, neither be polluted any more with all their transgression; but that they may be my people, and I may be their God, saith the Lord God," 8c., 11 v. We have here the facts as they have transpired and as they will continue to transpire in relation to this subject. The death of the prophet is one fact that has been realized although he abhorred and repented of this iniquity before his death. This branch of the subject we shall leave to some of our brethren, who are qualified to explain it satisfactorily. Those who have practiced these abominations have become "a sign and a proverb" among men in accordance with this prophecy. These are the "false teachers" prophesied of by Peter, of whom he said "many shall follow their pernicious ways; by reason of whom the way of truth shall be evil spoken of. And through covetousness shall they with feigned words make merchandise of you; whose judgment now

---

[23] The inspired translation reads: "I the Lord have not deceived that prophet."

of a long time lingereth not, and their abomination slumbereth not." The reason why the Lord destroyed the prophet and made those who "set up their idols in their heart," a sign and a proverb, made them bear the punishment of their iniquity is worthy of our earnest attention. We are informed that the reason why the Lord would perform all these things was this, "that the house of Israel may go no more astray from me, neither be polluted any more with all their transgressions; but that they may be my people, and I may be their God." Here is positive evidence that this prophecy was to be fulfilled in the last days, for there has only been a small part of the house of Israel (at any time since this prophecy was given) that were obedient to the Lord. The time is not fully come when Israel shall "go no more astray," and not "be polluted any more with all their transgressions," therefore the punishment of these men who have committed these sins must continue until that happy day shall come. But as the Lord says in this prophecy, "repent and turn yourselves from your idols; and turn away your faces from your abominations, so say we, and return unto the fold from whence you have strayed." As some may yet doubt whether God would act in this way toward men who set up their idols in their heart, we will see how God dealt with Balaam. In Numbers 22 c. we are informed that Balak, king of the Moabites, sent the elders of Moab and Midian unto Balaam with the rewards of divination in their hands to entreat him that he would curse Israel, but God said unto Balaam, "Thou shalt not go with them; thou shalt not curse the people, for they are blessed." And Balaam rose up in the morning, and said unto the Princes of Balak, "Get you unto your land; for the Lord refuseth to give me leave to go with you." And Balak sent yet again princes, more, and more honorable than they. And they came to Balaam and said to him, "Thus sayeth Balak, the son of Zippor, let nothing, I pray thee, hinder thee from coming unto me: For I will promote thee unto very great honor, and I will do whatsoever thou sayest unto me; come, therefore, I pray thee, curse me this people." Now although the Lord had said unto Balaam, "Thou shalt not go with them; thou shalt not curse the people, for they are blessed," yet the great honor that was offered him, allured him, and he inquired of the Lord again, and said unto the princes, "Tarry ye also here this night, that I may know what the Lord will say unto me more." And God came unto Balaam at night, and said unto him, "If the men come to call thee, rise up and go with them: but yet the word which I shall say unto thee, that shalt thou do." And Balaam rose up in the morning and saddled his ass, and went with the princes of Moab. And God's anger was kindled because he went; and the angel of the Lord stood in the way for an adversary against him. So we find that the Lord told him not to go, but afterwards, having "set up his idol in his heart" he inquired of the Lord again whether he might not go and curse Israel and God's anger was kindled against him because he did so, although God had commanded him to go. This is, therefore, a parallel case with Ezekiel's prophecy.[24]

In I Kings, 22 c. we are informed that the King of Israel wanted Jehoshaphat, king of Judah, to go up with him to Ramoth-Gilead to battle, and there were four hundred prophets who said "Go up, for the Lord shall deliver it into the hands of the king." And Jehoshaphat said, "Is there not here a prophet of the Lord besides, that we might inquire of him?" And the king of Israel said unto Jehoshapat, "There is yet one, Micaiah, the son of Imlah, by whom we may inquire of the Lord; but I hate him, for he doth not prophesy good concerning me, but evil." And Jehoshaphat said, "Let not the king say so." So he was sent for. The messenger that was gone to call Micaiah spake unto him, saying, "Behold now the words of the prophets declare good unto the king with one mouth: let thy word, I pray thee, be like the word of one of them, and speak that which is good." And Micaiah said, "As the Lord liveth, what the Lord saith unto me, that will I speak." We are then informed that Micaiah prophesied like the false prophets,[25] and then against them. And he said, "I saw the Lord sitting on his throne, and all the hosts of heaven standing by him on his right hand and on his left. And the Lord said, Who shall persuade Ahab that he may go up and fall at Ramoth-Gilead? And one said on this matter, and another said on that manner. And there came forth a spirit and stood before the Lord and said, I will persuade him. And the Lord said unto him wherewith? And he said, I will go forth, and I will be a lying spirit in the mouth of all his prophets. And he said, thou shalt persuade him, and prevail also; go forth and do so. Now therefore behold the Lord hath put a lying spirit in the mouth of all these thy prophets, and the Lord hath spoken evil concerning thee." This doctrine was extensively preached in the Church before iniquity overthrew the Church, and by this doctrine the Church might have been saved, if men had not "set up their idols in their heart."

---

[24] Mr. Sheen forgets that the Lord said, "Thou shalt not curse the people, for they are blessed," which command Balaam hearkened to.

[25] The prophecy was; "Go and prosper; for the Lord shall deliver it into the hands of the king," v. 15. This was uttered in mockery, if not why did the king reply: "How many times shall I adjure thee that thou tell me nothing but that which is true in the name of the Lord," v. 16. *Then* Micaiah told the king that he should fall at Ramoth-Gilead, so the king acted with full knowledge of the word of the Lord concerning his death when he went forth to battle. Therefore the Lord did not deceive Ahab in this matter.

INTRODUCTION OF CELESTIAL AND PLURAL MARRIAGE

Additional testimony of a few out of the multitude[26] of witnesses who were taught these principles by the Prophet Joseph Smith, and who knew that he received the revelation known as section 132 in the Book of Doctrine and Covenants.

AFFIDAVIT OF PRESIDENT LORENZO SNOW

In the month of April, 1843, I returned from my European mission. A few days after my arrival at Nauvoo, when at President Joseph Smith's house, he said he wished to have some private talk with me, and requested me to walk out with him. It was toward evening. We walked a little distance and sat down on a large log that lay near the bank of the river. He there and then explained to me the doctrine of plurality of wives; he said that the Lord had revealed it unto him, and commanded him to have women sealed to him as wives; that he foresaw the trouble that would follow, and sought to turn away from the commandment; that an angel from heaven then appeared before him with a drawn sword, threatening him with destruction unless he went forward and obeyed the commandment.

He further said that my sister Eliza R. Snow had been sealed to him as his wife for time and eternity. He told me that the Lord would open the way, and I should have women sealed to me as wives. This conversation was prolonged, I think one hour or more, in which he told me many important things.

I solemnly declare before God and holy angels, and as I hope to come forth in the morning of the resurrection, that the above statement is true.

Lorenzo Snow.

---

[26] One hundred or more affidavits in relation to the introduction of celestial and plural marriage are on file in the historian's Office, Salt Lake City, and are the expressions of eye and ear witnesses, who know that the Prophet Joseph Smith introduced and taught celestial and plural marriage. Most of these witnesses are members of the Church, but some of them are not, and have not been connected with the Church from before the martyrdom of the Prophet and Patriarch. It would be impracticable and even unnecessary to produce all this evidence here. A portion should suffice, in order that the truth regarding the introduction of these principles should be established; for, in this case as in all others, the testimony of two or three reliable witnesses should establish the truth of these things. Celestial marriage, which is marriage for eternity, should not be confused with plurality of wives, as is often done by those not acquainted with these teachings.

Territory of Utah,
Box Elder County. } ss.

Personally came before me J. C. Wright, Clerk of the County and Probate Courts in and for the County and Territory aforesaid, Lorenzo Snow, and who being duly sworn deposeth and says that the foregoing statement by him subscribed is true of his own certain knowledge.

Witness my hand and seal of Court, at my office in Brigham City, Box Elder County, Utah Territory, this 28th day of August, A.D. 1869.

[Seal.]   J. C. Wright, Clerk.

AFFIDAVIT OF LUCY WALKER

United States of America,
State of Utah.
County of Salt Lake.

Lucy Walker Smith Kimball, being first duly sworn, says:

I was a plural wife of the Prophet Joseph Smith, and was married for time and eternity in Nauvoo, State of Illinois, on the first day of May, 1843, by Elder William Clayton. The Prophet was then living with his first wife, Emma Smith, and I know that she gave her consent to the marriage of at least four women to her husband as plural wives, and she was well aware that he associated and cohabited with them as wives. The names of these women are Eliza and Emily Partridge, and Maria and Sarah Lawrence, all of whom knew that I too was his wife.

When the Prophet Joseph Smith mentioned the principle of plural marriage to me I felt indignant, and so expressed myself to him, because my feelings and education were averse to anything of that nature. But he assured me that this doctrine had been revealed to him of the Lord, and that I was entitled to receive a testimony of its divine origin for myself. He counseled me to pray to the Lord, which I did, and thereupon received from Him a powerful and irresistible testimony of the truthfulness and divinity of plural marriage, which testimony has abided with me ever since.

On the 8th day of February, 1845, I was married for *time* to President Heber C. Kimball, and bore to him nine children. And in this connection allow me to say to his everlasting credit that during the whole of my married life with him he never failed to regard me as the wife for eternity of his devoted friend, the Prophet Joseph Smith.

Lucy Walker Smith Kimball.

Subscribed and sworn to before me, this 17th day of December, 1902.

[Seal.]   James Jack, Notary Public.

AFFIDAVIT OF CATHERINE PHILLIPS SMITH

United States of America,
State of Utah.
County of Salt Lake.

Catherine Phillips Smith,[27] being first sworn, says:

I am the daughter of Thomas Denner and Sarah Godshall Phillips, and was born in Philadelphia, State of Pennsylvania, on the first day of August, 1819. My present residence is East Jordan, Salt Lake County, Utah.

I was married to Hyrum Smith, brother of the Prophet Joseph Smith, as his plural wife, and lived with him as his wife. The sealing was performed by the Prophet Joseph Smith himself, in Nauvoo, State of Illinois, in August, 1843, in the brick office belonging to my husband, and occupied at the time as a dwelling by Brother and Sister Robert and Julia Stone, and was witnessed by my mother, Sister Stone and her daughter Hettie.

In consequence of the strong feeling manifested at the time against plural marriage and those suspected of having entered into it, I, with my mother, moved to St. Louis near the close of the year, where I was living when the Prophet Joseph and my husband were martyred.

The purpose of this affidavit is that my testimony to the truthfulness and divinity of plural marriage may live after I shall have passed away; and in this spirit I commend it to all to whom it may come.

Catherine Phillips Smith.

Subscribed and sworn to before me, this 28th day of January, 1903.

[Seal.]   L. John Nuttall, Notary Public.

AFFIDAVIT OF ALMIRA W. JOHNSON SMITH BARTON

Territory of Utah,
County of Iron.   } ss.

Be it remembered on this first day of August A.D. 1883, personally appeared before me John W. Brown a notary public in and for said county, Almira W. John-

[27] Some time during the month of September four members of the Reorganized Church called on Catherine Phillips Smith at her home in East Jordan, with the object in view of having her deny her testimony regarding her marriage to the Patriarch Hyrum Smith, which she resolutely refused to do.

In a statement given on September 24th, two days before her death, she said: "They tried to get me to tell a lie and deny that I was married to the Patriarch Hyrum Smith; but I would not do it. I never have lied and will not now; my affidavit is true. They asked me if my mother knew of my marriage, and I told them that the Patriarch asked my mother if she was willing for him to marry her daughter, and she said he could ask the daughter, and she could do as she pleased. I told them that the Prophet Joseph sealed me to the Patriarch Hyrum Smith as his wife for time and all eternity, and they tried to get me to deny it, and I would not do it, for it is true. I told them the truth. They annoyed me very much, and I finally told them to leave my house and never enter it again."

son Smith Barton, who was by me sworn in due form of law, and upon her oath says: I am a citizen in the Territory of Utah, over the age of twenty-one years, and I am the daughter of Ezekiel Johnson and Julia Hills Johnson his wife; that I was born at Westford, in the State of Vermont on the 22nd day of October A.D. 1813; that I had nine brothers who were named respectfully Joel H., Seth, David, Benjamin F., Joseph E., Elmer, George W., William D., and Amos; and six sisters named respectfully Nancy, Dulcena, Julia, Susan, Mary and Esther, all of whom, with myself, were baptized into the Church of Jesus Christ of Latter-day Saints with the exception of Elmer, who died in infancy.

Deponent further says, that in the years 1842 and 1843, I resided most of the time at Macedonia, in the County of Hancock, State of Illinois, sometimes with my sister who was the wife of Almon W. Babbitt, and sometimes with my brother Benjamin F. Johnson. During that time the Prophet Joseph Smith taught me the principle of celestial marriage including plurality of wives and asked me to become his wife. He first spoke to me on this subject at the house of my brother Benjamin F. I also lived a portion of the time at Brother Joseph Smith's in Nauvoo, when many conversations passed between him and myself on this subject. On a certain occasion in the spring of the year 1843, the exact date of which I do not now recollect, I went from Macedonia to Nauvoo to visit another of my sisters, the one who was the widow of Lyman R. Sherman, deceased, at which time I was sealed to the Prophet Joseph Smith. At the time this took place Hyrum Smith, Joseph's brother, came to me and said I need not be afraid. I had been fearing and doubting about the principle and so had he, but he now knew it was true. After this time I lived with the Prophet Joseph as his wife, and he visited me at the home of my brother Benjamin F. at Macedonia.

Deponent further says that I had many conversations with Eliza Beaman who was also a wife of Joseph Smith, and who was present when I was sealed to him, on the subject of plurality of wives, both before and after the performance of that ceremony. And also that since the death of the Prophet Joseph Smith I was married for time to Reuben Barton of Nauvoo, Hancock Co., Ill., by whom I have had five daughters, one only of whom is now living.

Almira W. Johnson Smith Barton.

Subscribed and sworn to by the said Almira W. Johnson Smith Barton the day and year first above written.

[Seal.]John W. Brown, Notary Public.

AFFIDAVIT OF MARTHA MCBRIDE KIMBALL

Territory of Utah,
County of Millard. } ss.

Be it remembered that on this eighth day of July, A.D. 1869, personally appeared before me Edward Partridge, Probate Judge in and for said county, Martha McBride Kimball, who was by me sworn in due form of law, and upon her oath saith that sometime in the summer of the year 1842, at the city of Nauvoo, county of Hancock, state of Illinois, she was married or sealed to Joseph Smith, President of the Church of Jesus Christ of Latter-day Saints, by Heber C. Kimball, one of the Twelve Apostles in said Church, according to the laws of the same regulating marriage.

Martha McBride Kimball.

Subscribed and sworn to by said Martha McBride Kimball the day and year first above written.

[Seal.]   Edward Partridge, Probate Judge.

AFFIDAVIT OF MELISSA LOTT WILLES

Territory of Utah,
County of Salt Lake. } ss.

Be it remembered that on this twentieth day of May, A.D. 1869, personally appeared before me, James Jack a notary public in and for said county, Melissa Lott Willes, who was by me sworn in due form of law, and upon her oath saith that on the twentieth day of September, A.D. 1843, at the city of Nauvoo, county of Hancock, state of Illinois, she was married or sealed to Joseph Smith, President of the Church of Jesus Christ of Latter-day Saints, by Hyrum Smith, Presiding Patriarch of said Church, according to laws of the same, regulating marriage, in the presence of Cornelius P. Lott and Parmelia Lott.

Melissa Lott Willes.

Subscribed and sworn to by the said Melissa Lott Willes, the day and year first above written.

[Seal.]   James Jack, Notary Public.

LOVINA SMITH WALKER'S TESTIMONY

I, Lovina Walker, hereby certify that while I was living with Aunt Emma Smith, in Fulton City, Fulton Co., Illinois, in the year 1846, that she told me that she, Emma Smith, was present and witnessed the marrying or sealing of Eliza Partridge, Emily Partridge, Maria Lawrence and Sarah Lawrence to her husband, Joseph Smith, and that she gave her consent thereto.

Lovina Walker.

We hereby witness that Lovina Walker made and signed the above statement on this 16th day of June, A.D. 1869, at Salt Lake City, S. L. County, Utah Territory, of her own free will and record.

Hyrum S. Walker,
Sarah E. Smith,
Joseph F. Smith.

AFFIDAVIT OF SARAH A. KIMBALL

Territory of Utah,
County of Salt Lake. } ss.

Be it remembered that on this nineteenth day of June, A.D. 1869, personally appeared before me Elias Smith, Probate Judge for said county, Sarah Ann Kimball, who was by me sworn in due form of law, and upon her oath saith that on the twenty-seventh day of July, A.D. 1842, at the city of Nauvoo, county of Hancock, state of Illinois, she was married or sealed to Joseph Smith, President of the Church of Jesus Christ of Latter-day Saints, by Newell K. Whitney, Presiding Bishop of said Church, according to the laws of the same regulating marriage, in the presence of Elizabeth Ann Whitney her mother.

Sarah A. Kimball.

Subscribed and sworn to by the said Sarah Ann (Whitney) Kimball, the day and year first above written.

E. Smith, Probate Judge.

AFFIDAVIT OF ELIZABETH A. WHITNEY

Territory of Utah,
County of Salt Lake. } ss.

Be it remembered that on this thirtieth day of August, A.D. 1869, personally appeared before me, James Jack, a notary public in and for said county, Elizabeth Ann Whitney, who was by me sworn in due form of law, and upon her oath saith that on the twenty-seventh day of July, A.D. 1842, at the city of Nauvoo, county of Hancock, state of Illinois, she was present and witnessed the marrying or sealing of her daughter Sarah Ann Whitney to the Prophet Joseph Smith, for time and all eternity, by her husband Newel K. Whitney then Presiding Bishop of the Church.

E. A. Whitney.

Subscribed and sworn to by the said Elizabeth Ann Whitney the day and year first above written.

James Jack, Notary Public.

AFFIDAVIT OF ORSON HYDE

Springtown, Sept. 15, 1869.

I, Orson Hyde, do hereby certify and declare according to my best recollection that on the fourth day of September I was married to Miss Marinda N. Johnson, in Kirtland, Ohio, in the year of our Lord 1834, and in the month of February or March, 1843, I was married to Miss Martha R. Browitt, by Joseph Smith, the martyred prophet, and by him she was sealed to me for time and for all eternity in Nauvoo, Ill., and in the month of April of the same year, 1843, I was married by the same person to Mrs. Mary Ann Price, and by him she was sealed to me for time and for all eternity, in Nauvoo, Ill., while the woman to whom I was first married was yet living, and gave her cordial consent to both transactions, and was personally present to witness the ceremonies.

Orson Hyde.

Sworn to and subscribed to before me this the 15th day of September, 1869, at Springtown, Sanpete County, UT.

George Brough, Justice of the Peace.

I hereby certify that the above named George Brough is a justice of the peace for the precinct of Springtown in the county of Sanpete, UT., and that he is duly qualified in accordance with law; in testimony whereof, I hereunto set my hand and official seal of the County Court of Sanpete County, at my office, Manti City, this Sept. 16, 1869.

[Seal.]   William T. Reed, County Clerk.

AFFIDAVIT OF JOSEPH BATES NOBLE

Territory of Utah,
County of Salt Lake. } ss.

Be it remembered that on the 26th day of June, A.D. 1869, personally appeared before me, James Jack, a notary public in and for said county, Joseph Bates Noble, who was by me sworn in due form of law, and upon his oath saith, that on the fifth day of April, A.D. 1841, at the city of Nauvoo, County of Hancock, State of Illinois, he married or sealed Louisa Beaman to Joseph Smith, President of the Church of Jesus Christ of Latter-day Saints, according to the order of celestial marriage revealed to the said Joseph Smith.

Joseph B. Noble.

Subscribed and sworn to by the said Joseph Bates Noble, the day and year first above written.

[Seal.]   James Jack, Notary Public.

AFFIDAVIT OF RHODA RICHARDS SMITH

Territory of Utah,
County of Salt Lake. } ss.

Be it remembered that on this first day of May, A.D. 1869, personally appeared before me, Elias Smith, Probate Judge for said county, Rhoda Richards, who was by me sworn in due form of law and upon her oath saith that on the twelfth day of June A.D. 1843, at the city of Nauvoo, County of Hancock, State of Illinois, she was married or sealed to Joseph Smith, President of the Church of Jesus Christ of Latter-day Saints, by Willard Richards, one of the Twelve Apostles of said Church, according to the laws of the same regulating marriage.

Rhoda Richards.

Subscribed and sworn to by the said Rhoda Richards, the day and year above written.

[Seal.]   Elias Smith, Probate Judge.

TESTIMONY OF BENJAMIN F. JOHNSON

Mesa City, Arizona, 9th March, 1904.

President Joseph F. Smith,
Washington, D. C.

My Dear Brother:—

In reading reports from the Senate Committee on the Reed Smoot case, I see that witnesses are subpoenaed to prove that the Prophet Joseph Smith did not authorize or practice polygamy; and I do know that he did teach plural marriage, and that he did give to me a plural wife who is still living with me, and that I saw one of my sisters married to him. * * *

And I do know that at his Mansion House was living Mariah and Sarah Lawrence and one of Cornelius P. Lott's daughters as his plural wives with the full knowledge of his wife, Emma, of the married relations to him.

At that time I was his legal business agent at Macedonia or Ramtis, and was familiar with his family or domestic affairs; and occupying, as I did, the family mansion often in a business way with Emma, the Prophet's first wife, who at no time did ever in my hearing deny the plural character of her husband's family.

And now with this and much more knowledge relating to this subject, could my evidence before the Senate Committee be of any real value to the cause of truth? If so, although too infirm to travel alone I would willingly try to be there, if according to your counsel and wish.

Loyal to the truth, I am,

Always brother,
B. F. Johnson.

THE CELESTIAL AND PLURAL MARRIAGE REVELATION

The following letter was written by Elder William Clayton who wrote the revelation known as section 132 in the Book of Doctrine and Covenants, at the direction of the Prophet Joseph Smith, July 12, 1843.[28]

Salt Lake City, Nov, 11, 1871.

Madison M. Scott, Esq.

Dear Sir:

Your letter of 23rd of June last, was received by due course of mail, but owing to my being so very closely confined with public duties, which has almost destroyed my health, I have not

[28] This, however, was not the time this principle was first made known to the Prophet Joseph Smith, for as early as 1831 the Lord revealed the principle of celestial and plural marriage to him and he taught it to others.

answered your letter so promptly as is my practice. My health is yet very poor, but I have resigned the office which was bearing so heavy upon me, and am in hopes to regain my usual sound health.

Now, in regard to the subject matter of your letter, it appears to me that the principal topic is what is commonly called polygamy, but which I prefer to call celestial marriage. As to young Joseph saying that the Church here have apostatized; that *we* have introduced polygamy, denying bitterly that his father ever had a revelation on the subject, that is all mere bosh! I *believe* he knows better, and I have often felt sorry to learn that the sons of the Prophet should spend their time in contending against a pure and holy principle which their father's blood was shed to establish. They will have a heavy atonement to make when they meet their father in the next world. They are in the hands of God, and my respect for their father will not permit me to say much about the wicked course of his sons.

Now, I say to you, as I am ready to testify to all the world, and on which testimony I am most willing to meet all the Latter-day Saints and all apostates, in time and through all eternity, I did write the revelations on celestial marriage given through the Prophet Joseph Smith, on the 12th of July, 1843.

When the revelation was written there was no one present except the Prophet Joseph, his brother Hyrum and myself. It was written in the small office upstairs in the rear of the brick store which stood on the banks of the Mississippi river. It took some three hours to write it. Joseph dictated sentence by sentence, and I wrote it as he dictated. After the whole was written Joseph requested me to read it slowly and carefully, which I did, and he then pronounced it correct. The same night a copy was taken by Bishop Whitney, which copy is now here (in the Historian's office) and which I know and testify is correct. The original was destroyed by Emma Smith.

I again testify that the revelation on polygamy was given through the prophet Joseph on the 12th July, 1843; and that the Prophet Joseph both taught and practiced polygamy I do positively know, and bear testimony to the fact. In April, 1843, he sealed to me my second wife, my first wife being then living. By my said second wife I had two sons born in Nauvoo. The first died; the second is here now, and is married.

I had the honor to seal one woman[29] to Joseph under his direction. I could name ten or a dozen of his wives who are now living in this territory, so that for any man to tell me that Joseph

---

[29] See affidavit of Lucy Walker Smith.

did not teach polygamy, he is losing his time, for I know better. It is not hearsay, nor opinion with me, for I positively know of what I speak, and I testify to the truth, and shall be willing to meet all opponents on the subject through all eternity.

As to the Church here having apostatized that is all a mere matter of assertion, destitute of truth. President Young and his associates are, and have been doing everything they can to carry out the plans and instructions of the Prophet Joseph, and so eternity will prove to the condemnation and confusion of all their enemies. Any one who says to the contrary does not know Joseph nor the mission the Lord gave him to fulfill. * * *

Truly yours,
William Clayton.

AFFIDAVIT OF HOWARD CORAY

Territory of Utah,
County of Salt Lake.   } ss.

As many false statements have been made in relation to the authorship of the revelation on celestial marriage, I deem it but justice to all lovers of truth for me to express what I know concerning this very important matter.

On the 22nd day of July, A.D. 1843, Hyrum Smith, the martyred Patriarch, came in a carriage to my house in Nauvoo; he invited me and my wife to take a ride with him; accordingly, as soon as we could make ourselves ready, we got into his carriage and he set off in the direction of Carthage. Having gone a short distance, he observed to us that his brother Joseph Smith, the Prophet, had received a revelation on marriage, that was not for the public yet, which he would rehearse to us, as he had taken pains to commit it to memory. He then commenced rehearsing the revelation on celestial marriage not stopping till he had gone quite through with the matter. After which he reviewed that part pertaining to plurality of wives, dwelling at some length upon the same, in order that we might clearly understand the principle. And on the same day (July 22, 1843,) he sealed my wife, formerly Martha Jane Knowlton, to me; and when I heard the revelation on celestial marriage read on the stand in Salt Lake City, in 1852, I recognized it as the same as that repeated to me by Brother Hyrum Smith. Not long after this I was present when Brother David Fullmer and wife were sealed by Brother Hyrum Smith, the martyred Patriarch, according to the law of celestial marriage. And, besides the foregoing, there was quite enough came within the compass of my observation to have fully satisfied my mind that plural marriage was practiced in the city of Nauvoo.

Howard Coray.

Subscribed and sworn to before me, this 18th day of June, A.D. 1882.

[Seal.]   James Jack, Notary Public.

AFFIDAVIT OF DAVID FULLMER[30]

Territory of Utah,   } ss.
County of Salt Lake.

Be it remembered that on this fifteenth day of June, A.D. 1869, personally appeared before me, James Jack, a notary public in and for said county, David Fullmer, who was by me sworn in due form of law, and upon his oath saith, that on or about the 12th day of August, A.D. 1843, while in meeting with the High Council [he being a member thereof] in Hyrum Smith's brick office, in the City of Nauvoo, County of Hancock, State of Illinois, Dunbar Wilson made inquiry in relation to the subject of plurality of wives, as there were rumors about respecting it, and he was satisfied there was something in those rumors, and he wanted to know what it was. Upon which Hyrum Smith stepped across the road to his residence, and soon returned bringing with him a copy of the revelation on celestial marriage given to Joseph Smith July 12, 1843, and read the same to the High Council, and bore testimony to its truth. The said David Fullmer further saith that, to the best of his memory and belief, the following named persons were present: William Marks, Austin A. Cowles, Samuel Bent, George W. Harris, Dunbar Wilson, William Huntington, Levi Jackman, Aaron Johnson, Thomas Grover, David Fullmer, Phineas Richards, James Allred and Leonard Soby. And the said David Fullmer further saith that William Marks, Austin A. Cowles and Leonard Soby were the only persons present who did not receive the testimony of Hyrum Smith, and that all the others did receive it from the teachings and testimony of the said Hyrum Smith; and further, that the copy of said revelation on celestial marriage published in the *Deseret News* extra of September 14, A.D., 1852, is a true copy of the same.

David Fullmer.

Subscribed and sworn to by the said David Fullmer the day and year first above written.

[Seal.]   James Jack, Notary Public.

AFFIDAVIT OF LEONARD SOBY[31]

Be it remembered that on the 23rd day of March, in the year 1886, before, Joshua W. Roberts, notary public for the City of Beverly, County of Burlington, State of New Jersey, Leonard Soby, of said city, county and state, was by me duly sworn, and upon his oath saith:

That on or about the 12th day of August, 1843, I was a resident of Nauvoo, Hancock County, State of Illinois, and being a member of the High Council of the Church of Jesus Christ of Latter-day Saints, was present at a meeting of said council at the time herein above stated; Thomas Grover, Alpheus Cutler, David Fullmer, William Huntington and others; when Elder Hyrum Smith, after certain explanations, read the revelation on celestial marriage.

[30] Similar affidavits by most of the members of this High Council at Nauvoo are also on file.

[31] Leonard Soby was at first opposed to this revelation, and shortly after the martyrdom he left the Church. When this statement was given he was not a member of the Church.

I have read and examined carefully said revelation, since published in the Book of Doctrine and Covenants of said Church, and say to the best of my knowledge and belief it is the same, word for word, as the revelation then read by Hyrum Smith.

The deponent says further, that the revelation did not originate with Brigham Young, as some persons have falsely stated, but was received by the Prophet Joseph Smith, and read in the High Council by his authority as a revelation to the Church of Jesus Christ of Latter-day Saints.

When read to this deponent and said High Council, I believed it was a revelation from Jesus Christ, and I believe so now.

Leonard Soby.

Subscribed and sworn to by the said Leonard Soby the day and year first above written.

Joshua W. Roberts, Notary Public.

Witnessed by:
James H. Hart,
Samuel Harrison.

AFFIDAVIT OF JOHN W. RIGDON

Territory of Utah,
County of Salt Lake. } ss.

John W. Rigdon, being duly sworn, says: I am the son of Sidney Rigdon, deceased. Was born at Mentor, in the State of Ohio, in the year 1830, and am now over seventy-five years of age. My father, Sidney Rigdon, joined the Church of Jesus Christ of Latter-day Saints that year, and was in 1833 ordained to be Joseph Smith's first counselor which position he held up to the time Joseph the Prophet was killed, at Carthage jail, in 1844. That Joseph Smith and Sidney Rigdon moved from Kirtland, with their families, to the State of Missouri, during the winter of 1837, but Rigdon did not reach Far West, in the State of Missouri, until the last of April, 1838. That during the troubles in Missouri, in the year 1838, Joseph Smith, Hyrum Smith, his brother, Sidney Rigdon, Lyman Wight and others, whose names I do not now remember were arrested and imprisoned in Liberty jail, about forty miles from the village of Far West, in Caldwell County, Missouri, where they all remained incarcerated for several months. That while said Joseph Smith, Hyrum Smith, Sidney Rigdon, Lyman Wight and others were prisoners in said Liberty jail, as aforesaid I, with my mother, wife of Sidney Rigdon, Emma Smith, wife of said Joseph Smith, and Joseph Smith, son of Joseph and Emma Smith, went to see the said prisoners during the latter part of the winter of 1838. We all went together in the same carriage and came home together. We stayed at Liberty jail with the prisoners three days and then left for home. The story that is being told by some of the members of the Reorganized Church, at Lamoni, that young Joseph Smith, now president of the said Reorganized Church, was ordained by his father, Joseph Smith, to be the leader of the Church of Jesus Christ of Latter-day Saints after his father's death, is not true, for I know that no such ordination took place while we were at Liberty jail; that if any such ordination had taken place I most certainly should have known it and remembered it, as I was with young Joseph, the Prophet's son, all the time we were there. If Joseph Smith had ordained his son Joseph to be the leader of the Church at his death, he would have done so in a manner that there could have been no doubt about it. Both of his counselors were then in prison with him, namely, Sidney Rigdon and Hyrum Smith, and it would have been in order for the prophet to have called upon them to assist him in such an ordination had it taken place, and a record of the same made in the Church books, so that all members of the Church might have known that such an ordination had taken place. But nothing of the kind appears in the Church books. My father and mother lived a good many years after the incarceration at Liberty jail, and I, who lived near my father, never heard my father or my mother mention that such an ordination ever took place in Liberty jail; and as I know myself that no such ordination took place in Liberty jail, and inasmuch as it is not claimed that an ordination of this character was bestowed at any other place, therefore I deny it as an untruth and a story gotten up by the Reorganized Church for effect.

Besides all this, if Joseph Smith, the President of the Reorganized Church was ordained while in Liberty jail, why did he, sixteen years after his father's death, receive an ordination under the hands of William Marks, William W. Blair, and Zenas H. Gurley? Would it not seem that one ordination (and that too, said to have been by his own father, the President of the Church) should have been sufficient? But further Wm. Marks, Wm. W. Blair and Zenas H. Gurley had all been excommunicated from the Church of Jesus Christ of Latter-day Saints (excepting William W. Blair, who never belonged to it) before they "ordained" young Joseph to be President of the Reorganized Church, and therefore they did not have the authority to ordain him. The whole story of his being ordained by anyone having authority to do so is too preposterous to be entertained for a single moment, and should be rejected by all who hear such a story mentioned.

As to the truth of the doctrine of polygamy being introduced by the Prophet Joseph Smith, deponent further says: Joseph Smith was absolute so far as spiritual figures were concerned, and no man would have dared to introduce the doctrine of polygamy or any other new doctrine into the "Mormon" Church at the city of Nauvoo during the years 1843 and 1844, or at any other place or time, without first obtaining Joseph Smith's consent. If anyone had dared to have done such a thing he would have been brought before the High Council and tried, and if proven against him, he would have been excommunicated from the Church, and that would have ended polygamy forever, and would also have ended the man who had dared to introduce such a doctrine without the consent of the Prophet Joseph.

And deponent further says: Joseph the Prophet, at the City of Nauvoo, Illinois, some time in the latter part of the year 1843, or the first part of the year 1844, made a proposition to my sister, Nancy Rigdon, to become his wife. It happened in this way: Nancy had gone to Church, meeting being held in a grove near the temple lot on which the "Mormons" were then erecting a temple, an old lady friend who lived alone invited her to go home with her, which Nancy did. When they got to the house and had taken their bonnets off, the old lady began to talk to her about the new doctrine of polygamy which was then being taught, telling Nancy, during the conversation, that it was a surprise to her when she first heard it, but that she had since come to believe it to be true. While they were talking Joseph Smith the Prophet came into the house, and joined them, and the old lady immediately left the room. It was then that Joseph made the proposal of marriage to my sister. Nancy flatly refused him, saying if she ever got married she would marry a single man or none at all, and thereupon took her bonnet and went home, leaving Joseph at the old lady's house. Nancy told father and mother of it. The story got out and it became the talk of the town that Joseph had made a proposition to Nancy Rigdon to become his wife, and that she refused him. A few days after the occurrence Joseph Smith came to my father's house and talked the matter over with the family, my sister, Mrs. Athalia Robinson also being present, who is now alive. The feelings manifested by our family on this occasion were anything but brotherly or sisterly, more especially on the part of Nancy, as she felt that she had been insulted. A day or two later Joseph Smith returned to my father's house, when matters were satisfactorily adjusted between them, and there the matter ended. After that Joseph Smith sent my father to Pittsburgh, Pa., to take charge of a little church that was there, and Ebenezer Robinson, who was then the Church printer, or at least had been such, as he was the printer of the paper in Kirtland, Ohio, and a printer by trade, was to go with him to print a paper there, and nine days before Joseph Smith was shot at Carthage we started, reaching Pittsburgh the day before he was killed.

Deponent further says: I have in my possession a paper called the *Nauvoo Expositor*, bearing date, Nauvoo, Illinois, Friday, June 7th, 1844, which said paper's printing plant was destroyed by the City Council at Nauvoo a night or two after that issue. There never was but one issue of this paper. Joseph Smith the Prophet was then Mayor of the City of Nauvoo. In the afternoon of the day on which the printing plant was destroyed, Henry Phelps, a son of W. W. Phelps, came down Main Street selling this paper, the *Nauvoo Expositor*, and everyone who could raise five cents bought a copy. In that paper the three following affidavits appeared, which I reproduce herewith.

AFFIDAVITS

I hereby certify that Hyrum Smith did (in his office) read to me a certain written document which he said was a revelation from God. He said that he was with Joseph when it was received. He afterwards gave me the document to read and I took it to my house and read it and showed it to my wife and returned it the next day. The revelation (so called) authorized certain men to have more wives than one at a time in this world and in the world to come. It said this was the law, and commanded Joseph to enter into the law. And also that he should administer to others. Several other items were in the revelation, supporting the above doctrines.

Wm. Law.

State of Illinois,
Hancock County.

I, Robert D. Foster, certify that the above certificate was sworn to before me as true in substance, this fourth day of May, A.D. 1844.

Robert D. Foster, J. P.

I certify that I read the revelation referred to in the above affidavit of my husband. It sustained in strong terms the doctrine of more wives than one at a time in this world and in the next. It authorized some to have to the number of ten, and set forth that those women who would not allow their husbands to have more wives than one should be under condemnation before God.

Jane Law.

Sworn and subscribed before me this 4th day of May, A.D. 1844.

Robert D. Foster, J. P.

To all whom it may concern:

Forasmuch as the public mind hath been much agitated by a course of procedure in the Church of Jesus Christ of Latter-day Saints by a number of persons declaring against certain doctrines and practices therein (among whom I am one) it is but meet that I should give my reasons at least in part as a cause that hath led me to declare myself. In the latter part of the summer of 1843, the Patriarch Hyrum Smith did in the High Council, of which I was a member, introduce what he said was a revelation given through the Prophet, that the said Hyrum Smith did essay to read the said revelation in the said council; that according to his reading there was contained the following doctrines: 1st. The sealing up of persons to eternal life, against all sins save that of shedding innocent blood or of consenting thereto; 2nd. The doctrine of plurality of wives or marrying virgins; that David and Solomon had many wives, yet in this they sinned not, save in the matter of Uriah. This revelation with others, evidence that the aforesaid heresies were taught and practiced in the Church, determined me to leave the office of first counselor to the President of the Church at Nauvoo, inasmuch as I dared not teach or administer such laws. And further deponent saith not.

Austin Cowles.

State of Illinois,
Hancock County.

To all whom it may concern: I hereby certify that the above certificate was sworn and subscribed before me, this fourth day of May, 1844.

Robert D. Foster, J. P.
John W. Rigdon.

Sworn to before me this 28th day of July, 1905.

[Seal.]   James Jack, Notary Public.

STATEMENT OF ORANGE L. WIGHT

The following confirmation of John W. Rigdon's affidavit is copied from the *Deseret News* of Saturday, August 12, 1905:

Bunkerville, Lincoln County, Nev., August 4, 1905:—Seeing the testimony of J. W. Rigdon in the semi-weekly *News* of July 31, and being much interested in the subject, and knowing that there lived in this place a man that was quite familiar with the early scenes of church history, especially those in and about Far West, Missouri, and having heard him say that he had many times visited his father and the Prophet Joseph, while they were incarcerated in Liberty jail, I went and interviewed Orange L. Wight (eldest son of former Apostle Lyman Wight), who is now 82 years old and resides with his daughter, Sister Harriet M. Earl. Brother Wight is quite feeble in body, but his mind seems to be as bright as ever.

I found Brother Wight in his usual good humor, and seemed quite willing to talk, in fact, was pleased to do so. "Elder Wight," said I, "are you willing to make a statement for publication in regard to what you know about Joseph Smith, son of the Prophet Joseph, being ordained while in Liberty jail to lead the Church?" "Certainly I am." "Then," said I, "just write me out a brief statement covering those points, and I will give it in your own words." Following is Brother Wight's statement:

"In regard to the statement of John W. Rigdon, I endorse it in every point. Brother John W. Rigdon speaks of being in Liberty prison when the Prophet Joseph Smith, Sidney Rigdon, Hyrum Smith, Lyman Wight, and others were there (the others were Caleb Baldwin and Alexander McRae). I also visited the prisoners at or about the same time, and slept with them many times at different periods, and I cannot recollect of ever hearing the subject of an ordination mentioned.

"My father, Lyman Wight, nor my mother, never alluded to it during their lifetime in my presence; so I take it for granted that Joseph, the son of the Prophet Joseph Smith, was not ordained to fill the place of his father, in the Liberty jail. I was born in the State of New York, November 29, 1823, hence am about seven years older than Brother John W. Rigdon. And if an ordination of Young

Joseph had occurred in the prison, I would likely have heard it, and would certainly recollect it.

"Previous to this, while I was several years younger, the Twelve Apostles were organized and commissioned to assist in leading and governing the Church. I can recollect every detail distinctly. My acquaintance with the Prophet was from the year 1830 to his martyrdom, and I can truly say he was a Prophet of God, and was appointed to the divine mission to organize the Church of Jesus Christ of Latter-day Saints in this last dispensation.

"As to the Prophet's believing and practicing polygamy, I have as near a certain knowledge of the fact, I may say, as any man living. I was well acquainted with most or all of his wives, and talked with them on the subject, at the same time my wife also talked with them.

"If there is anything further that is necessary for me to communicate in regard to my recollection, I will willingly do so.

"Respectfully,
"Orange L. Wight."

Further talk with Brother Wight brought out the following facts: He was baptized into the Church in the spring of 1832; was with the Church through all their troubles in the State of Missouri. Brother Wight filled a thirteen months' mission in the State of Virginia in company with Jedediah M. Grant and others; was in Nauvoo at the time the Prophet was captured at Dixon, Ill., and was one of those who went up the Illinois river on the steamer "Maid of Iowa," to assist in rescuing the Prophet.

Joseph I. Earl.

AFFIDAVIT OF BATHSHEBA W. SMITH

State of Utah,   } ss.
County of Salt Lake.

Bathsheba W. Smith, being first duly sworn on oath, deposes and says:

I was a resident of Nauvoo, State of Illinois, from 1840 to 1846. I was married to George A. Smith July 25, 1841, Elder Don Carlos Smith performing the ceremony. Near the close of the year 1843, or in the beginning of the year 1844, I received the ordinance of anointing in a room in Sister Emma Smith's house in Nauvoo, and the same day, in company with my husband, I received my endowment in the upper room over the Prophet Joseph Smith's store. The endowments were given under the direction of the Prophet Joseph Smith, who afterwards gave us lectures or instructions in regard to the endowment ceremonies. There has been no change, to my certain knowledge, in these ceremonies. They are the same today as they were then. A short time after I received my anointing, I was sealed to my husband, George A. Smith, for time and eternity, by President Brigham Young, in the latter's house, according to the plan taught, to my knowledge, by the Prophet Joseph Smith. When I was married in 1841, I was married for time, and not for eternity.

At the time I was anointed in Sister Emma Smith's house, she (Emma Smith) said in my presence, to me and to others who were present upon that occasion, "Your husbands are going to take more wives, and unless you consent to it, you must put your foot down and keep it there." Much more was said in regard to plural marriage at that time by Sister Emma Smith, who seemed opposed to the principle.

In the year 1840, at a meeting held in Nauvoo, at which I was present, I heard the Prophet Joseph Smith say that the ancient order would be restored as it was in the days of Abraham. In the year 1844, a short time before the death of the Prophet Joseph Smith, it was my privilege to attend a regular prayer circle in the upper room over the Prophet's store. There were present at this meeting most of the Twelve Apostles, their wives, and a number of other prominent brethren and their wives. On that occasion the Prophet arose and spoke at great length, and during his remarks I heard him say that he had conferred on the heads of the Twelve Apostles all the keys and powers pertaining to the Priesthood, and that upon the heads of the Twelve Apostles the burden of the Kingdom rested, and that they would have to carry it.

It has been, and is, necessary for me to make this statement, as contrary reports have been circulated as coming from me. Any statements purporting to come from me that have been made, or that may be made by any party or parties, in opposition or conflicting with this sworn statement, are false, as I have never, to my knowledge, deviated one iota from this statement.

Bathsheba W. Smith.

Signed in the presence of
Joseph F. Smith, Jr.,
B. Morris Young.

Subscribed and sworn to before me this 19th day of November, 1903.

[Seal.]   Martin S. Lindsay, Notary Public.

THE REORGANIZED CHURCH—SOME FACTS REGARDING ITS ORIGIN

The ministers of the "Reorganized" Church, or the "New Organization," as it was first called,[32] declare that the Church at the death of the Prophet Joseph and Patriarch Hyrum Smith, was badly divided, its members scattered to the four winds, and that the Church was rejected with its dead. They also claim that the "Reorganization" is composed of the faithful who did "not bow the knee to Baal," but remained true to the "original faith" as revealed and practiced by the Prophet Joseph Smith. In the words of their president: "The individuals who kept this covenant (the new and everlasting covenant) were accepted of Him and were not rejected, nor their standing before God put in jeopardy by the departure of others from the faith. Whatever the office in the priesthood each held, under the ordinations ordered by the call of God and vote of the Church, would remain valid. They could as elders, priests, etc., pursue the duties of warning, expounding, and inviting all to come to Christ, and by command of God could build up the Church from any single branch, which, like themselves, had not bowed the knee to Baal, or departed from the faith of the Church as found in the standard works of the body at the death of Joseph and Hyrum Smith."[33]

It is strongly implied in this quotation from the writings of the president of the "Reorganization" that all those who followed President Brigham Young and the Twelve Apostles, lost their Priesthood and standing before the Lord, and that the founders of the "New Organization" and their followers were the only ones who remained true and steadfast to the Truth. The evidence in this regard is against them. The truth is that the founders of the "Reorganized" church were the ones who followed every will-o-the-wisp, bowed the knee to Baal and departed from the faith, while the Twelve and the Saints on the other hand, pursued an even course and were steadfast under all trials and difficulties even to the end.

It is not true that the Church was broken, scattered and rejected following the martyrdom and that the "Reorganization" is a portion of the original church. Their organization did not come into existence until some sixteen years after the death of the Prophet and Patriarch and was an outgrowth of the movement under James J. Strang.

There was a movement on foot to divide the Church, following the assassination of the Prophet and Patriarch, but its range was not as extensive as has generally been supposed. The chief actors in this movement were Sidney Rigdon, James J.

[32] *Saints' Herald*, Vol. one.
[33] See article in *Era*, Vol. 7, No. 11, entitled, "The Church Rejected—When?"

Strang and William Smith, each of whom aspired to lead the Church. Mr. Rigdon based his claim to the presidency on the fact that he had been the first counselor to the Prophet Joseph Smith, and therefore by right should be the "guardian" of the Church. His claim was in conflict with the position of the Church and the teachings of the Prophet. He laid his case before the conference of the Church August 8, 1844, and his claim was rejected by the Saints almost unanimously. At the same conference the Twelve Apostles were sustained as the presiding quorum of the Church. Mr. Strang's claim to the presidency was based on his statement that the Prophet had appointed him as his successor by letter, a few days before the martyrdom. William Smith claimed the right of presidency by virtue of being the brother of the Prophet.

Each of these men gathered around him a few followers, principally of that class of restless, erratic individuals, who never remain contented very long in any one place or under any circumstances; but none of them gathered many followers. Their organizations barely existed for a few years and then disappeared; the fragments becoming the nucleus of the "Reorganization."

The movement which resulted in the bringing forth of the "Reorganized" church, was of more recent date and was due principally to the efforts of two men, viz., Jason W. Briggs and Zenas H. Gurley. Mr. Briggs was born June 25, 1821, at Pompey, Oneida County, New York. He joined the Church June 6, 1841, and members of the "Reorganization" declare that he was ordained an Elder in 1842. His home was in Beloit, Wisconsin, from 1842 to 1854. After the death of the Prophet, Mr. Briggs sustained the Twelve Apostles and the Church and was apparently true to them until the exodus in 1846. At that time he lost heart, turned from the Church in its darkest hour and sought the favor of the world. Some time subsequent to this he joined the movement under James J. Strang. In Strang's organization he did missionary work, received honors and organized a branch. In 1850 he renounced Mr. Strang and joined with William Smith, in the latter organization he was "ordained" an "apostle." He soon tired of William Smith, and in 1851 joined with Zenas H. Gurley who was at that time a follower of James J. Strang. These two men then organized a church of their own which afterwards was known as the "Reorganized" church. In 1886 Jason W. Briggs withdrew from this organization of his own begetting, declaring that it was not the Church of Christ.

Zenas H. Gurley was just as unstable as Mr. Briggs. He was born at Bridgewater, New York, May 29, 1801, joined the Church in April, 1838, and moved to Far West, from whence he was driven with the Saints in the expulsion of 1838-39. After this expulsion he settled in Nauvoo, where, in 1844, he was ordained a Seventy,[34] under the direction of President Joseph Young, and on the 6th day of April, 1845, he was ordained senior president of the twenty-first quorum of Seventy. He sustained the Twelve and followed their teachings and remained with the Church until February, 1846, (the month of the exodus) when he also left the Church and

---

[34] The "Reorganized" Church History states that Z. H. Gurley was ordained a Seventy in Far West in 1838. This is an error, they have no original record of such an ordination. The original records of the Seventies in the Historian's Office, Salt Lake City, give his ordination as stated here.

shortly afterwards joined with James J. Strang. Mr. Gurley was endowed in the Nauvoo Temple with his wife January 6, 1846, and of that event the record of Seventies states under date of January 10, 1846:

> President Zenas H. Gurley arose and said that the Presidents of the quorum (21st) had received their endowment. He observed that it was remarkable for the unusual outpouring of the Holy Spirit.—Page 29.

Again speaking of the authorities of the Church he said:

> He remembered forcibly the sayings of the First Presidents of Seventy, that we should so live that no charge can be brought against us. A few years ago the men in high standing in this Church were as little as we are. They obtained their exaltation by patient submission to right, and minding their own business.—Page 29.

On January 25th, 1846, he said:

> The Saints who have passed through the trials of the Church were generally rooted and grounded in love and have a witness in their own hearts or they would not have remained.—Page 33.

Within a very few days of this time Zenas H. Gurley deserted the Church because he was unable to face the trials and hardships the Saints were forced to undergo. The "Mormon" people were journeying in a strange land, the prospects before them were dark and some of the members became faint-hearted and were unable to endure to the end. Of this number Jason W. Briggs and Zenas H. Gurley were two who turned back and sought refuge in the apostate organization of James J. Strang. Indeed it required a strong heart and a firm-rooted faith for men and women to give up all earthly comforts and undertake a journey of that kind. Death stared the Saints in the face, they were poorly clothed, without shelter, save their ragged tents that would not shed the rain, and almost destitute of food; yet with the exception of the few who sought the "flesh-pots of Egypt," they patiently and determinedly pursued their way until crowned with the victory. The opinion of the world at that time was that the exodus meant the end of "Mormonism," and that the Latter-day Saints had gone to their destruction; for without the necessary means to support life, and isolated as they were from the rest of civilization, they must surely perish in the barren and distant West. Such, too, would doubtless have been the case had not the protecting hand of Jehovah guided them. Is it any wonder under such trying conditions that the hearts of those weak in the faith should fail them?

In 1849 Mr. Gurley filled a mission for Mr. Strang and made a number of converts to that faith. In 1850 he organized the "Yellowstone branch," for the Strangite church. In 1852 he rejected the claim of Mr. Strang and joined with Mr. Jason W. Briggs, and these two men united their respective Strangite branches, those of Yellowstone and Beloit, and organized themselves into a new religious movement known today as the "Reorganized" church. In 1853, the leaders of this movement called a number of men to the ministry, "ordained" seven "apostles" and began a proselyting movement. For several years they tried to get "young Joseph," the son of the Prophet Joseph Smith, who had never affiliated with the Saints since the exodus from Nauvoo, to join them and become their president. In this they failed, but were diligent and finally, through their continued efforts and the persuasion of his mother, he accepted that position in 1860, was "ordained" president of their church by William Marks, Zenas H. Gurley, and William W. Blair, and has continued in that position ever since.

Mr. Gurley remained with this movement till his death, but his family, together with Jason W. Briggs, voluntarily withdrew in 1886.

In 1852, when Jason W. Briggs and Zenas H. Gurley combined their Strangite forces the membership was about one hundred souls, most of whom were converts made for Mr. Strang. In 1860, when "young Joseph" assumed the leadership, the membership was three hundred souls, most of whom were converts that had never belonged to the Church of Jesus Christ of Latter-day Saints.

Of the members of the Church who were in fellowship in 1844-46, the "Reorganization" has received no more, and likely less than one thousand converts, which fact shows that the apostasy was not so great in 1844-46, as has been pictured. These statements are based on the testimony of original members of the "Reorganization," as they testified before the U. S. Court of Appeals for the Western District of Missouri, in 1894, in the Temple Lot suit, which was for the possession of property in the hands of the "Church of Christ" or "Hedrickites."

Before that court Mr. William W. Blair, who for many years was a member of the presidency of the "Reorganization" and who was one of its oldest members, testified that "one thousand was probably too high an estimate for the members of the original church, that had joined the Reorganized church." He could "approximately say" that one thousand had joined the "Reorganized church, and possibly that estimate was too large." Record pp. 180, 181.

William Marks, whose testimony is referred to by Mr. Evans, was also one of those who joined the "Reorganization" in an early day. At the time of the martyrdom he was president of the Nauvoo Stake, but was disfellowshipped for transgression at the October conference, 1844, and finally excommunicated. Afterwards he joined the organization under James J. Strang. In that organization he became a "bishop," was a member of the "high council," and later a member of the "first presidency." After the death of James J. Strang, he joined the organization of Charles B. Thompson, another apostate. This is the same William Marks who "ordained" Joseph Smith, of Lamoni, president of the "Reorganization." In that ordination he was assisted by Zenas H. Gurley and William W. Blair. Mr. Blair never belonged to the Church. It is almost needless to add that these men held no divine authority and could not bestow the Priesthood and officiate in the ordinances of the Gospel, and, therefore, the pretentions of the "Reorganized" church are fraudulent. Judged by its history, doctrines and the unstable character of its founders it is proved to be a counterfeit and nothing more.

Considering the conditions under which the "Reorganization" came into existence, and the fact that in the beginning the original one hundred members came from the Strangite church, and that during the existence of that organization from its foundation to 1894, not more than one thousand members of the "original church" (i.e. the Church of Jesus Christ of Latter-day Saints as it stood in 1844) had joined it, we are not to be blamed if we declare that that church is not the successor, a faction or a portion of the "original church" founded by Joseph Smith the Prophet through the command of God, April 6, 1830. And after following the history of its founders and pointing out their instability and the manner in which they followed after false leaders, receiving "ordinations" and honors under their hands, we can most emphatically declare that they were not the faithful who did "not bow the knee to Baal," and who kept the "everlasting covenant."

Lector House believes that a society develops through a two-fold approach of continuous learning and adaptation, which is derived from the study of classic literary works spread across the historic timeline of literature records. Therefore, we aim at reviving, repairing and redeveloping all those inaccessible or damaged but historically as well as culturally important literature across subjects so that the future generations may have an opportunity to study and learn from past works to embark upon a journey of creating a better future.

This book is a result of an effort made by Lector House towards making a contribution to the preservation and repair of original ancient works which might hold historical significance to the approach of continuous learning across subjects.

HAPPY READING & LEARNING!

LECTOR HOUSE LLP
E-MAIL: lectorpublishing@gmail.com